ASTRO-PSYCHOLOGY

A synthesis of Jungian psychology and astrology
showing how, with Jung's principle of
synchronicity, the zodiacal signs and planets
influence the basic dispositions and psychic make-
up of the individual.

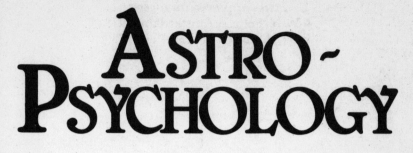

ASTRO-PSYCHOLOGY

*Astrological Symbolism and the
Human Psyche*

by

KAREN HAMAKER-ZONDAG
Translated from the Dutch by Transcript

SAMUEL WEISER INC.
734 Broadway, New York, N.Y. 10003

First published in Holland as
Psyche en astrologisch symbool
© W.N. Schors, Amsterdam, 1978
First published in English in 1980

© THE AQUARIAN PRESS 1980

ISBN 0 87728 465 2 (USA)

Printed in Great Britain

Contents

Foreword

Astrology has fascinated me ever since I first encountered it. It has enabled me to see myself and the people and things around me in a different light. Above all, it has helped me to a better understanding of human behaviour and of events and situations.

At the same time, I have been bothered by occasional questions to which there were no satisfactory answers. Whenever, in the extensive astrological literature, characteristic behaviour and events are assigned to certain planets, signs, houses etc., I could not refrain from asking myself why one thing is said to go with another. In particular, it is when we come to human conduct that so many problems crop up. Why do the same astrological factors work out in one way with one person and in another way with someone else? What mechanisms are at work in a horoscope regarded as a picture of the psychic structure of an individual?

During the period when these questions were occupying my mind, I was studying the psychology of Prof. Carl G. Jung, and I gradually discovered that many of the concepts he had introduced and had utilized in his practice were very similar in content to the more symbolic idiom of astrology. I was then faced with the challenge of fitting Jung's concept into the existing astrological world of ideas without doing violence to either. A great deal of inspiration was derived at this time from a number of lessons given by Rob Nederveen-Pieterse, which put me on the track of the relationship between the structure of the psyche and the house structure of the horoscope. If you turn to Chapter 6 of this book, you will see what I eventually made of it. Anyway, I owe him a big debt of thanks.

This book is the outcome of my attempt to find a place for

Jungian psychology within an astrological framework. I hope that the attempt will result both in the dynamics of psychology gaining an entry into astrology and astrology winning wider recognition. Perhaps, psychologists too will see the value of astrology as a practical tool.

My thanks are due to Maggie Schors and to my husband, Hans, both of whom displayed angelic patience in commenting on the style and content of my manuscript. Their constructive criticism and the many discussions we have had have proved to be invaluable.

Amsterdam, June 1978

1

Psychology and Astrology: An Introduction

In order to grasp the true meaning of alchemy and astrology, it is necessary to have a clear conception of the inner relationship and identity of the microcosm and the macrocosm and of their interaction. All the forces in the universe are potentially present in man and in the body of man, and all human organs are nothing else than the products and representatives of nature's powers.

Paracelsus

A Psychological Approach

Astrology is one of the earliest attempts made by man to find the order hidden behind or within the confusion and apparent chaos that exists in the world. The human race learnt to relate the experiences of life to the ordered pattern disclosed by the circling heavens. And so, astrology became a symbolic language with sufficient vitality to survive right down to our own times; with enough flexibility to develop with the race itself. Its ancient framework seems to agree wonderfully with modern psychological concepts, especially those used in the theories of the eminent psychiatrist, Prof. Jung. Thanks to his own insights and to those of his many followers, it is possible to give an up-dated interpretation to much of the content of the astrological symbols; all the more so as Jung's findings and intuitions often hark back to the original experiences of mankind enshrined by so many cultures in their scriptures, traditions, mythologies and fairy tales.

Over and over again, certain motifs seem to be given prominence in the legends and nursery stories of world literature. These motifs seem to be almost universal and are often found, even today, in fantasies and dreams, in the hallucinations of fever patients and in the delusions of the mentally deranged. Carl Jung sifted through these and many other phenomena for materials with which to construct a working model of the human psyche and, in doing so, he drew the highly important distinction between personal consciousness, the personal unconscious and the collective unconscious. The conscious and the unconscious are two complementary spheres displaying opposite characteristics. They balance one another, so to speak. But Jung's opinions on the unconscious were completely different from those of his former teacher Sigmund Freud. In Freud's view, the unconscious mind is where material repressed by the individual is stored, and he gave the name 'preconscious' to that layer of the mind from which we have instant recall. Jung's term 'personal unconscious' essentially covers both of the above concepts of Freud; his 'preconscious' and his 'unconscious'.

In addition, Jung introduced the new expression, 'collective unconscious' to denote a compartment of the psyche whose contents are not specific to our individual Egos or the result of personal experience, but derive from the inherited structure of the brain and from the inherited potential of psychic functioning in general. It is conceived of as incorporating all the types of psychic reaction and all human experiences right from the very beginning of mankind. This is the reason for using the word 'collective'. The assumption is made that we are all part of one another and that we share this unconscious mind with all our fellow men. Within the collective unconscious lies the source of those motifs which the whole world has in common, motifs which, as we have already seen, can also play an important role in the individual psyche. How this process takes place is explained by Jung in a detailed analysis of the collective unconscious.

Archetype and the Collective Unconscious

Just as we inherit our physical characteristics from our parents and ancestors, so we inherit archetypes as the material of the collective unconscious; an inheritance we share with the rest of mankind. The meaning of the word 'archetype' has been much disputed because, in the main, its true significance has not been grasped. Jung himself offered the following definition:

The archetype is a formal element, empty in itself, which is nothing more than a *facultas praeformandi*, an *a priori* possibility of the form in which the idea appears. It is not our ideas themselves that are inherited but merely their forms, which, in this respect, are the exact equivalents of the equally formally determined instincts. Nor can the archetypes, any more than the instincts, be shown to be present as such, until they are brought to concrete manifestation .

We have seen that the collective unconscious, as the repository of all archetypes, contains every human experience from man's earliest days. It is certainly no storehouse of dead material; quite the reverse. It forms the matrix of our behaviour and reactions. Nevertheless, we are still in the dark as to the origin of the archetypes; their nature remains inscrutable. We can get to know them only when they are manifested as images in our psyches, but we must not make the mistake of thinking that these images are the archetypes themselves. It is difficult to frame a precise definition of the concept 'archetype' because, in addition to a conscious content, it has an unconscious content which is not easy to put into words. At best, an archetype can be compared to a 'root idea' or 'disembodied idea' already in existence before it is clothed in a material form; just as the potential for crystal formation is present in a chemical solution before the commencement of crystallization. We infer that the potential is there already but recognize it only by its expression in a material form. The same is true of archetypes. The form is there in potential, before the psychic content is shaped into thoughts or mental images. In the deepest sense, an archetype is unchangeable, it can however reveal itself in countless different ways.

Archetypes are governing principles in the hidden part of the human psyche; they are force fields and force centres which serve to marshal whatever items sink into the unconscious. Their activities lie outside our field of consciousness but exert a great effect on what we do or refrain from doing. 'Indeed', says Jolande Jacobi, 'all life expressions, in so far as they are of a general human and typical sort, rest on an archetypal foundation, no matter whether they manifest themselves on the biological, the psycho-biological or the mental level.'

A clear distinction must be made between archetype in the sense of the potentiality for taking form and archetype in the sense of a possibility which had already taken form – the archetypal image. The literature often emphasizes the latter. This has been one of the many sources of confusion which bedevil an already elusive idea. The many guises under which the archetypes appear also create difficulties, the impression being given that the term archetype is a convenient pigeon-hole for everything in the human psyche that defies explanation. This impression is helped by the tendency to label many ideas as archetypes while losing sight of the difference between what Jung calls the 'archetype as such' and the archetypal image. The so-called 'archetype' refers to no more than one of the modes of manifestation of the 'archetype as such' in many cases. This confusion between the primary idea and its forms of expression also occurs in the writings of Carl Jung himself. He was using the broad term archetype as early as 1919 but did not stumble upon the essential distinction until 1946. In anything he wrote before his article 1946 the reader himself must work out whether he is talking about the 'archetype as such' (i.e. the real archetype) or about an archetypal manifestation (i.e. an archetype which has become an image).

Thus, the 'Archetype of the Mother', which is stored in the collective unconscious under no given form, can reveal itself in the human soul in innumerable ways. It is impossible to discuss the mother archetype in all its depth, but a few of the possibilities for its manifestation will be mentioned here by way of illustration. One of the primary principles of the mother archetype is the idea of the maternal, the cherishing, the providing and the protecting. Growth and the giving of form also fall within the scope of this archetype, for the embryo forms in the womb, and is completely enveloped and protected by the mother. Each object or idea that gives man a feeling of safety and security can therefore be seen as a symbol for the archetype of the mother. The Church may be seen as an example of how the archetype of the mother becomes an image, because the Church gives spiritual safety and protection to the believers. Other examples are the Motherland and Mother Earth. The feeling of being sheltered by anything in which we happen to be enclosed (like a child in the womb) gives hollow forms such as a cave, a yoni or the womb itself the power to stand as a symbol for the inborn archetype of the maternal. Thus in dreams, a cave, while it could perhaps refer to the dreamer's mother, could just as well represent the idea of motherhood.

Tied up with this problem of drawing a distinction between the archetype itself and its manifestation, is the question of whether or not comparatively few archetypes serve as the source of the vast numbers of archetypal images. If not, we are presumably faced with an endless series of archetypes. Jolande Jacobi has this to say about it:

Each archetype can develop and differentiate endlessly. It can branch like a tree and blossom a thousandfold. There seems to be no answer to the question of whether there are many primitive impulses-to-form, i.e. archetypes. In the last analysis, we can fall back on the possibilities inherent in typical fundamental experiences. Who knows? Maybe they can be reduced to a unity consisting of two basic opposites such as light and dark or heaven and earth, the groundwork of creation itself. The deeper the layer at which a given archetype lies in the unconscious, the simpler will be its metaphorical language and the more meaning will reside within it waiting for unfoldment and, therefore, the more significant it will be.

Symbols in Astrology

Every archetype as such is a potential symbol, which means to say that the form it takes when manifesting itself can be represented by a symbol. For instance, the mother archetype can be symbolized as a fountain, a yoni etc. Thus each symbol is determined by an archetype which is not perceptible in itself. It *must* have this archetypal basis in order to qualify as a symbol although it need not be positively identical with the archetype. Each archetype as such can materialize as a symbol at any time, providing a general psychic constellation or conformable situation is present in the consciousness. In essence, an archetype is a compressed centre of psychic energy and the symbol is attached to it to make it visible. With this in mind, Jung described a symbol as an 'aspect and image of psychic energy'. In other words, the unconscious supplies us, so to speak, with archetypal forms which are empty in themselves and beyond our conception, and then the conscious mind fills them out with similar or related imagery so bring them within our grasp.

Goethe has given a striking description of the notion of symbolism, which, according to him, is near enough as follows: 'Symbolism converts a phenomenon into an idea and an idea into an image in such a way that the idea is endlessly active yet unattainable in the image. Even when expressed in all languages, it remains inexpressible'. According to Carl Jung, the use of symbolism presupposes that the chosen expression is the best possible designation or formula for a more or less unknown reality, the existence of which is admitted or, at any rate, thought desirable. On the one hand, symbols express the inner psychic process in a representative manner and, on the other hand, after the image has been formed, they impress themselves on this process and so carry forward the stream of psychic events.

Someone once dreamed that it was spring but that, in the garden, the branches of his favourite tree were bare. That year it bore neither leaves nor blossoms. This withered life-tree had risen out of his unconscious mind as a symbol for the fact that the person was leading a very intellectual life and had lost contact with his natural instincts. Thus, not only did the symbol present the dreamer with a certain message in picture form, but this remonstrance also made an impression on him and enabled him, by responding to the dream and its symbolism, to modify the direction of his psychological development.

In this connection, it should be mentioned that a symbol is essentially different in content from a 'sign'. The latter is always an expression which is put in the stead of a known cause. A good example is given by Jung himself in his *Psychological Types* : the winged wheel on the cap of a railway worker does not symbolize the railways, it is merely a sign that he is on the railway staff. In this instance, the wheel is a short way of indicating something that is completely known to the conscious mind. As a sign, it is a simplified indication or analogy of what is familiar. On the other hand, a symbol always contains something impossible to express in speech – that tool of reason. The Dutch word for symbol, *zinnebeeld*, makes this rather clear. Literally, it means a 'sense picture'. The symbol as *zin*, i.e. 'sense' or 'meaning', is connected with the rational side of the psyche resident in consciousness and, as *beeld*, i.e. 'picture', it is connected with the contents of the unconscious. Whereas a sign is just a synonym, a symbol is an allegory: it stands for something beyond what is known.

The whole astrological world of ideas can be interpreted as a meaningfully ordered assembly of symbols, necessarily resting on an archetypal foundation. We have seen that archetypes compose the collective unconscious common to all men. The signs of the zodiac, the planets, houses, etc. can be rediscovered in everyone's psyche; they are archetypes which have assumed definite forms, representatives of psychic material and processes which man has learned to cope with through the long centuries. Using the heavens as an analogy, he has constructed a symbolic language. He has gazed into the sky to find patterns in which to embody the archetypal entities welling up from deep inside him, patterns he recognized as the most accurate expression of his experiences and feelings.

However, whether or not something is felt to be a symbol, entirely depends on the attitude adopted by the observer's conscious mind. The intellect can regard a given reality both as *itself* and as a *vehicle* for conveying what is hitherto unknown. Nevertheless, it is possible for the consciousness to reject the symbolic nature of a given reality, in spite of a consensus of opinion to the contrary. Because the variety of symbols is so great, some of them are bound to be ordinary, everyday objects. A tree, for example, can be regarded either as a purely natural phenomenon (in which case, it is not a symbol) or as standing for something other that itself, such as a human life. In addition to symbols taken from the real world, there are those which have no direct connection with experience via the sense-organs but are pictures having a symbolic force of their own. Jung's famous example is that of the eye in the triangle. Since such things do not correspond to everyday reality, one is compelled to look for their symbolic significance, though this is not to say that everyone automatically does so. A great deal depends on what Jung calls the symbolic frame of mind, a concept he elucidates as follows in his *Psychological Types* :

Symbols which do not possess their own symbolic force as explained here (reference is made to the example of the eye in the triangle), either are dead, i.e. replaced by a better formula, or are productions whose symbolic character rests on the standpoint taken by the conscious mind of the observer. For the sake of brevity, we can term this standpoint (which treats a given phenomenon as a symbol) 'the symbolic frame of mind'. It finds its justification only partly in the actual state of affairs because, to a greater or lesser extent, it is the outcome of a philosophy which tends to attach meaning to events and imparts to the meaning a value higher than that possessed by the bare fact itself. The contrasting approach is that which always lays emphasis on objective facts and subordinates any meaning to these facts. There can, in general, be no symbols in the latter approach where symbolism stems entirely from the manner in which things are considered.

Symbols which are not representations of actual things, obtrude their symbolic character on the observer so to speak, but it depends on the observer whether the symbol is 'living' or not. If the symbol has a deeper meaning for the person concerned, it comes alive for him. By the same token, however, the symbol introduces him to historical or philosophical ideas in which it is no longer a symbol in the deepest sense of the word. So there will always be people who, because of their symbolic frame of mind, will be able to penetrate the world of symbols and discover the deeper significance of the phenomenal world. The symbolic language of astrology will appeal to and be understood by people of this type; in each case the signification becomes a symbol for them and this will be an aid in their own psychological development.

But there will always be individuals who have no appreciation of symbolism. To them, facts and phenomena have nothing behind them and remain as they appear in the tangible world of the senses. Those whose conscious mind is not influenced by symbolism will have little or no understanding of those who do live in a world of symbolism. Individuals of the first class will see the stars as nothing more than stars and, since they have no feeling for symbolism, will condemn the whole of astrology as nonsense. This is an understandable judgement when one considers the way their minds work. On the other hand, individuals whose minds are adapted to a symbolic mode of thought have even less comprehension of the first-mentioned. It is so hard for them to imagine that what to them is nothing more than a simple truth could seem untrue to others.

In these two psychologically opposed states of mind, with their totally different outlooks on the world, lies the deeper cause of the great controversy over 'belief' in astrology and its possible usefulness. Astrology presents few problems to those whose conscious minds are orientated towards symbolism, but for those not so orientated it appears to be an insurmountable stumbling block. We may therefore conclude that the great debate over the truth and demonstrability of astrology is not worth bothering about to any great extent. It depends on the cast of a person's conscious mind, whether he accepts astrology because he is at home with symbolism or rejects it because symbolism is foreign to him. To argue from opposite points of view can lead only to a hardening of attitudes and useless polarization, whereas tolerance and acceptance of the existence of another valid outlook can be a key to deeper insight into the phenomenon known as the 'human psyche'.

Synchronicity and Causality

The causality of our scientific view of the world divides everything up into simple events and, with great care, it tries to separate these events from all other parallel processes. For obtaining reliable data, this is absolutely necessary; but looked at from a global standpoint it has the disadvantage of obscuring, either in part or in the whole, the universal interrelationship of events. It has an increasingly adverse effect on the acquisition of knowledge concerning large-scale relationships and concerning the unity of the whole. For everything that happens, happens in the self-same world and belongs to it. On these grounds, events must possess an *a priori* aspect of unity.

So wrote Carl Jung, at the end of a long life, in his *Mysterium Coniunctionis*, after he had already amply discussed the enlightening principle of synchronicity in various books, papers and letters. In doing so, he repeats in essence the Great Law of Analogy discovered and employed in antiquity and expressed in the aphorism, 'that which is above is as that which is below'*, a principle which has always been basic to

---

*'*Quod est superius est sicut quod est inferius*'. A quotation from the alchemical *Smaragdine Table of Hermes*.   *Translator's note.*

astrology, right from early times. The revival of this old law within the framework of Western science, has proved to be of the utmost significance. It has enabled us to gain an insight into situations and events which seem to be inexplicable in terms of the principle of causality; that is, into those that appear not to come within the scope of cause and effect. There is no need to appeal to the principle of synchronicity when the law of cause and effect can show that a certain happening is the result of other, logically connected, happenings. However, where causality is no longer applicable and 'chance' intervenes, another way of explaining things is required. Jung formulated this on one occasion as follows: 'I discovered that there are psychic conformities, with no causal link between them, which must have another type of connection. It seems to me that the essential character of this connection is that the phenomena occur fairly simultaneously, hence the term "synchronistic"'. After prolonged experimentation by J.B. Rhine in the field of paranormal phenomena, it was clear to Carl Jung that 'our world-picture is in agreement with reality only if it makes room for improbabilities'.

The use of the term 'synchronicity' was a source of misunderstanding to many. In the first place, Jung was definitely not referring to a simultaneous coincidence of events; he was rather talking about a relative simultaneity which is comprehended only by a personal subjective experience. It is just this subjective element which is decisive, i.e. the relative simultaneity. However, of equally great importance is the meaningful content of what happens; in other words, it is the sense of experiencing a meaningful connection which welds events   which are not linked causally into a single whole. Jung deliberately avoided the use of the word *synchronism* to designate his newly discovered principle, preferring the word synchronicity to indicate that the simultaneity is relative.

Hence the definition of the principle of synchronicity contains two key concepts: the objective phenomenon of events occuring at more of less the same time without a causal connection between them, *and* the subjective factor in which the person himself must feel either that the events are a simple 'accident' which is devoid of point or meaning or that they form a very significant experience. And at this point the contrast between two human types which we have discussed above comes to the fore. The subjective element in the synchronistic principle makes it inevitable that not everyone will find significance in events which take place simultaneously and have a possibly meaningful connection.

The principle of synchronicity is not a philosophical notion but an empirical idea arising from the lack of any proper way of explaining the growing number of phenomena impossible to account for by cause and effect. Jung's explanation for the occurrence of synchronistic phenomena is that there is an active and *a priori* type of knowledge in the unconscious of man that rests on a corresponding arrangement of the microcosm and the macrocosm, in which the archetypes function as classifiers. The collective human unconscious, which we share with all our fellows, contains *everything*. It is built up of archetypes, and their existence is a prerequisite for the formation of everything which takes shape in our world of existence, in which they introduce a certain degree of order. If archetypes are really present in the human unconscious as autonomous, ordering factors, then Jung's hypothesis that the unconscious knows everything already is no more than logical.

The above-quoted correspondence between the microcosm and macrocosm, also supported by Jung, can be seen, too, as one way of putting the astrological principle that we can 'read' how the small events on earth take shape if we study the greater events in the heavens. But this again, presupposes a controlling principle over all, a transcendent 'entity', known to us as God, who is revered in all religions and cultures worthy of the name. This transcendent being is beyond the reach of our terms of reference – space and time – and therefore beyond human comprehension. Jung writes in his *Mysterium Coniunctionis*: 'This background to the universe as a whole partakes as much of the physical as of the mental sphere and so belongs to neither but rather is a third quantity, neutral in character, of which man can form only a vague idea at best, for in essence it is transcendental. ... Synchronicity points to a connectedness, yes even to a unity, of psychic and physical events which are not linked causally with one another. Hence it discloses an aspect of unity in Existence'.

With this principle and this description, Carl Jung hands to those whose conscious mind is habituated to symbolic thinking a key to a better understanding of the why and wherefore of this ancient science of astrology and, at the same time, supplies a modern explanation of principles which, before his time, were dismissed by many people as unimaginably old and effete 'magical' ideas.

2

The Astrological
World of Ideas

Tao brings forth one.
One brings forth two.
Two brings forth three.
Three brings forth the ten thousand things.
The ten thousand things bring forth the dark element without
and the light element within.

Tao Teh King XLII.

The One, the Life that is not knowable in itself, reveals itself in us human beings by means of an all pervasive life-force and life-impulse. In nature too, that Life is expressed in an infinite richness of forms of which man gradually becomes aware during the passage of time. Because forms and conditions keep changing and succeeding one another, man is able to make comparisons and note differences; and it is only by noting differences that he can assign significance and value to everything. So, someone who is ill learns to place a higher value on health and realizes that he cannot take it for granted. Seeing the two sides of a question can mean that it is understood and experienced more deeply and intensely. An individual has a greater appreciation of his physical condition when he has experienced the two extremes, sickness and health. The difference between sickness and health can be experienced only in the course of time, just as one gets to know Life itself as it presents one with contrasts in the course of time.

However, the apparent contrasts, such as sickness and health, really comprise a unity; in which case, we have two contrasting forms of expression of the *same* fundamental things, e.g. the above-mentioned physical condition of a person. Therefore, in what follows, we shall talk about contraries when a single matter or state of affairs is considered in its apparently opposed aspects. Our mental equipment being what it is, we have to have an antithesis between light and dark, hot and cold, full and empty etc. if we are to perceive them. Without sensory or mental perception no differences can be experienced and without the observation of differences consciousness is impossible. The apparent contrast of opposites lies at the root of our existence.

Astrology uses a range of ideas that individually and together represent various facets of that *one* Life. It has adopted, as a basic principle, the contrasts contained in these ideas. Ancient China already knew the opposites, Yin and Yang, which together make up the sum total of life. This fundamental idea has been taken up in the West as the contrasts male-female, light-dark, active-passive, creative-receptive, positive-negative and electric-magnetic. We know there is such a thing as light by beholding the contrast with darkness. Without light there is no darkness and without darkness no light. Both principles are equally necessary because we would fail to experience the one without the other.

Each sign of the zodiac, each planet, each house, each aspect, in short each element within the astrological frame of reference, is a two-sided unit. Although, following the traditional school, one side may be regarded as good and the other as bad, it is preferable to avoid thinking in these terms since they are 'loaded' with value judgements which make it impossible to penetrate to the heart of the contrasts. And, anyway, we can experience 'good' as good only because of the presence of evil and *vice versa*; although the actual judgements we make are purely subjective. Every concept used in astrology has its own specific positive and negative sides and learning and remembering both sides is essential for greater comprehension of, and insight into, ourselves and what is going on around us. Accepting and forming a union between these opposites or polarities which, as Richard Wilhelm put it, 'evoke one another', can eventually lead to inner harmony. In this connection, the Confucian saying 'Create inner harmony' is of crucial importance.

The Signs of the Zodiac

The earth and the other planets describe a path around the

sun. Looking at our solar system from the standpoint of its centre, the sun, gives us a heliocentric scheme, but in astrology a geocentric scheme is mainly employed, with the object of viewing the sun, moon and planets in their motions as seen from the earth. This has little to do with taking the earth to be the centre of our solar system; its motive is that the earth is the planet on which our lives are shaped. In fact, the horoscope is simply a diagram of the heavens as seen from a certain point on earth at a given moment of time; a diagram showing the exact positions of the sun, moon and planets, together with various astronomical points of intersection. This implies that the picture of the heavens for the time of some event, a birth say, does not deviate from astronomical reality even when geocentric. It is from this astronomical picture that the astrologer derives the details from his interpretation.

In addition to the rhythmic alternation of night and day due to the rotation of the earth on its own axis, we also experience the annual rhythm of the seasons. The seasons change because the earth makes a complete circuit round the sun each year and because, down the centuries, the earth maintains a practically constant angle of 66° 33' to the plane in which its circuit round the sun lies. In other words, wherever the earth happens to be in its circuit round the sun, its axis is always set at the same angle. (See Fig. 2.1). The consequence is that the sun does not remain perpendicular over the equator throughout the year, but the point where it is perpendicular at noon shifts backwards and forwards.

For one half of the year, the series of noon-points formed in this way moves into the Northern Hemisphere during the northern spring and summer and, in the other half of the year, it moves into the Southern Hemisphere. If we draw a continuous line through all these points, beginning with the spring point and moving on to where each succeeding point is found after a further rotation of the earth through 360° (or a sidereal day of 23 hours 56 minutes and 4 seconds), we obtain a projection on the terrestrial globe of the path apparently traced on the earth by the overhead noonday sun. This apparent path of the sun is known as the ecliptic.

Since the plane of the ecliptic makes an angle of 23° 27' with the plane of the equator, two points of intersection are formed. The first point where the sun is overhead at the

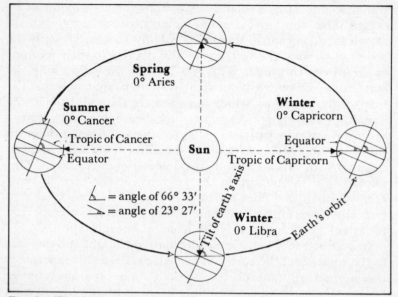

Fig. 2.1 The Seasons in the Northern Hemisphere as Determined by the Tilt of the Earth's Axis.

equator once a year is called the spring point (the first point of Aries). It is reached by the sun on the 21st March as it passes from the Southern to the Northern Hemisphere. This is the beginning of spring and through the whole of spring the sun climbs higher and higher in the sky in the Northern Hemisphere. On the 21st March day and night are of equal length but, as spring advances, the days get longer in the Northern Hemisphere and the intensity of the light and warmth increases; the reason being that the suns rays penetrate the earth's atmosphere by a shorter and shorter route because the angle at which they strike the earth becomes greater and greater. At one of the poles, in this case the North Pole, the area where the sun ceases to set increases in size. (See Fig. 2.3).

The high-point is reached when the sun culminates in the northern sky on the 21st June. The degree of latitude where the sun is then overhead at noon is known as the tropic of Cancer (although strictly speaking the sun only reaches its highest position at *one* point in this circle).

On this day too, the area surrounding the North Pole where

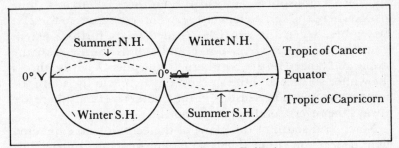

Fig. 2.2 The Apparent Path of the Sun or Ecliptic.

the sun does not set has reached its greatest extent and is bordered by the polar circle. However, from the moment the sun attains its northernmost position in 0° Cancer, it starts its descent. That is why we use the terms *tropic* (i.e. turning point) of Cancer and summer *solstice* (i.e. standing still of the sun), and this solstice is caller the *summer* solstice because it marks the commencement of summer in the Northern Hemisphere. The sun sinks lower and lower in the sky and the days get shorter and shorter until, on the 23rd September, the day and night are equal in length. The sun is then overhead at the equator or, to put it another way, the plane of the ecliptic cuts the plane of the equator at the autumn point (symbolically known as the first point of Libra). Autumn begins and, in the Northern Hemisphere, the nights become gradually longer. The sun now pursues a path over the

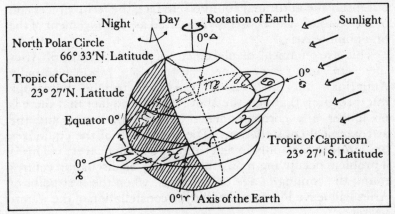

Fig. 2.3

Southern Hemisphere and, in the north polar area, a zone grows where the sun no longer rises. This continues to the 21st December, when the sun has receded to its furthest extent from the Northern Hemisphere and stands overhead at the tropic of Cancer in the Southern Hemisphere. To us, this is the winter solstice and the shortest day, while in the south the summer begins. The seasons in the Southern Hemisphere are always the reverse of those in the north.

North and south of the plane of the ecliptic and extending eight degrees on either side is a belt known as the zodiac. The zodiac is divided into twelve equal sectors of 30° each and these sectors are called the signs of the zodiac. Each sign has its own name taken from the name of the constellation which used to occupy it centuries ago. Hence a sign is not the same as a constellation. The constellations themselves (that is to say the group of stars to which our ancestors gave the names which were adopted by the signs in the distant past) are not of equal size; the signs, however, were eventually made equal and it is to the *signs* that human experience is related.

Another point which sometimes causes argument is the fact that the first point of *Aries*, in the sense of Aries the sign, is now in that part of the heavens occupied by the constellation *Pisces*. This displacement is due to the phenomenon known as the 'precession of the equinoxes'. We have an equinox when the sun is so placed in relationship to the earth that day and night are equal everywhere. This occurs *only* when the plane of the equator cuts that of the ecliptic, which is at the first point of Libra (the autumnal equinox). In fact, the term 'precession of the equinox' can be freely translated as 'displacement of the first point of Aries'.

This astronomical displacement of the first point of Aries the sign into Pisces the constellation (and eventually Aquarius) has little more relevance to the horoscope interpretation than has the above-mentioned fact that there is no longer any correspondence between the signs and the astronomical constellations. The precession of the equinoxes has a rôle to play only in determining astrological eras. This is a problem occupying many minds today as discussion centres round the coming of age of Aquarius, when the first point of Aries will leave Pisces and enter the constellation of the water-bearer.

However, in the first place astrology is a symbolic language based on centuries upon centuries of experience. All that is important is the meaning contained in the synchronous events recorded in the horoscope chart symbolically and experienced by man (as has already been discussed in Chapter I). In a letter he wrote in January 1934, Carl Jung gives a very clear explanation of this symbolic relationship:

> The astrological indication of time, 'the sun in Aries', is an expression of "spring" without reference to the actual zodiacal constellation in which the sun is placed. After several thousand years the sun, when it is in the sign we choose to call Aries, will really be in Capricorn astronomically speaking. In other words it will be in a constellation we associate with midwinter, and yet spring will have lost none of its force.

It appears that what Carl Jung calls the quality of the moment remains the same whether we speak of the sun in Aries, spring or the period running from the 21st March to the 21st April. He said that astrology was an example of synchronicity on a big scale, although he did not exclude the possibility of causal relationships. This is a possibility that he began to consider when, in 1951, Max Knoll made the following suggestion in his lecture on changes in modern science: the proton stream from the sun is so influenced by planetary conjunctions, oppositions and squares that the occurrence of electomagnetic storms (in sun spot periods) can be calculated in advance with a high degreee of certainty. It has already been found that periods of high sun spot activity correspond with peaks in the mortality curve for humans. There is also a correlation between electromagnetic storms on the sun and the intensity of radio interference. So Max Knoll made the assumption of causal relationships or objective influences of the planetary aspects on the proton radiation from the sun. Conjunctions, squares and oppositions had a patently unfavourable effect (a finding largely in keeping with traditional astrological ideas) whereas favourable effects could be ascribed to traditionally helpful aspects such as the sextile and trine.

This certainly points towards a causal relationship and, in 1958, Jung also wrote in a letter: 'As I have already observed, astrology seems to be in need of different hypotheses; I am not in a position to come out in favour of one or the other.' The reason for Jung's uncertainty was his opinion that synchronistic phenomena ought not to be predictable and Max Knoll's reasoning would not fit, therefore, into his thoroughgoing synchronistic conception of astrology. The results of J.B. Rhine's experiments later modified Jung's point of view in this respect in the sense that '... it is possible to calculate the statistical probability of the occurrence of synchronistic phenomena'. This means that no violence is done in any way to the essentially synchronistic basis of astrology.

The zodiac is the symbol for man's pathway through life and consists of the signs given in Fig. 2.4

The principle of opposites is found once more in each sign in their capacity for manifesting their contents either constructively or destructively. Then again, successive signs are treated as positive and negative. However, the words

English Name	Latin Name	Symbol	Alternative symbol
Ram	Aries	♈	
Bull	Taurus	♉	
Twins	Gemini	♊	
Crab	Cancer	♋	
Lion	Leo	♌	
Virgin	Virgo	♍	
Scales	Libra	♎	
Scorpion	Scorpio	♏	♏
Archer	Sagittarius	♐	
Sea-goat	Capricorn	♑	♑
Water-bearer	Aquarius	♒	
Fish	Pisces	♓	

Fig. 2.4 The Signs of the Zodiac

positive and negative must not be interpreted as meaning good and bad but more in the sense of the above-mentioned Yin and Yang, active and passive, male and female. From a psychological point of view, there is a great deal in common between the positive signs and extrovert behaviour and between the negative signs and introvert behaviour. The signs are alternately positive and negative, beginning with the positive sign Aries. This is followed by the negative sign Taurus, the positive sign Gemini and so on.

Besides its division into positive and negative signs, the zodiac is split up in two other ways, that is to say into quadruplicities (or crosses) and triplicities (or elements).

There are three quadruplicities, each containing four signs; which are the Cardinal Signs, the Fixed Signs, and the Mutable Signs. These signs are symbols of the various ways in which psychic energy can manifest. The law of opposites, which is the basis for the manifestation of life, demands a form of energy that is helpful in balancing its apparent polarities. Jung embodied these energy forms in his conception of the 'libido' (which he took to mean something altogether different from what Freud understood by the word) and used this term as an alternative for the expression 'psychic energy'. So the dynamics of the positive-negative polarity resides in the three quadruplicities, but the whole is expressed on earth in a fourfold manner, symbolized by the four elements, fire, earth, air and water.

Each quadruplicity is separately formed of four fundamentally differing attitudes or approaches to life (see Chapter 4), represented by the four elements. Each element has three signs, all three of which belong to a different quadruplicity. Therefore, all in all, we have twelve different signs making up the zodiac. Our results so far can be set out as follows.

Positive		Negative		
Fire	Air	Earth	Water	
Aries	Libra	Capricorn	Cancer	Cardinal
Leo	Aquarius	Taurus	Scorpio	Fixed
Sagittarius	Gemini	Virgo	Pisces	Mutable

Fig. 2.5 Classification of the Signs of the Zodiac

To sum up, we can say that the zodiac is split up into two groups of opposite polarity; the positive and negative signs. In each we distinguish three basic forms or directions of psychic energy. These are the quadruplicities, all three of which express themselves in four psychological functions with their corresponding human types (see Fig. 2.6). In Chapters 3 and 4, the significance of each of the quadruplicities and triplicities will be discussed in more detail and a link will be forged between these astrological ideas and modern psychological insights.

The Planets

The solar system consists of a number of planets, our moon and one star, the sun, which are all important from an astrological point of view. Although the sun and moon are not planets in an astronomical sense, they will be treated as such for the sake of simplicity.

Name	Symbol	Alternative symbols in use
Sun	☉	
Moon	☽	
Mercury	☿	
Venus	♀	
Mars	♂	♂
Jupiter	♃	
Saturn	♄	♄
Uranus	♅	♅ ♂
Neptune	♆	♆
Pluto	♇	P ♇ ☋ ♇
Earth	⊕	

Fig. 2.6 The Planets*

*The symbols have been rearranged slightly to give first place to those most usually found in English books.   *Translators note*

Everything in the cosmos is in a state of vibration. The atoms and molecules of all substances at a temperature above -273°C (the absolute temperature at which matter would fall apart) are in constant movement, even though the materials they constitute are solid and motionless. A good description of matter is 'congealed' energy or information. Planets, like the human body, are energies which have crystallized in a certain

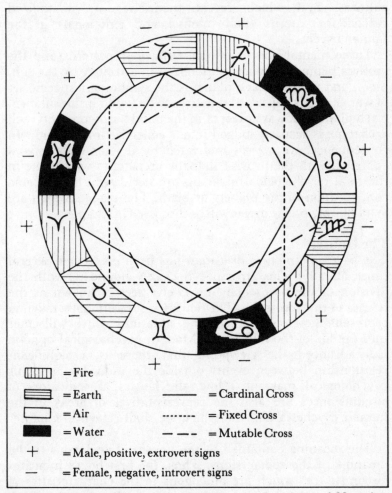

= Fire		
= Earth	———	= Cardinal Cross
= Air	········	= Fixed Cross
= Water	— — —	= Mutable Cross
+	= Male, positive, extrovert signs	
—	= Female, negative, introvert signs	

Fig. 2.7 The Classification of the Zodiac by Positive and Negative Signs, Triplicities and Quadruplicities

way according to a given pattern. Plato, when talking of 'the idea', had already grasped the principle of a pre-existing 'matrix': a basic idea which precedes, orders and determines its material expression.

This 'idea' exhibits a great measure of agreement with the psychological concept 'archetype' that, as we have already seen in Chapter 1, is synonymous with the basic images, held by us in common with men and women of all eras and cultures, and which reveal themselves in crystallized behaviour patterns (both mental and emotional) in the human psyche.

These mental and emotional behaviour patterns and the motives behind them are symbolized in astrology by the sun, moon and planets. Each planet is the symbol of a specific set of wants, needs, wishes and desires to be found inside all men. Each planet is always present in the natal horoscope and each archetype is securely lodged in our collective unconscious. In consequence, we are all motivated by the same archetypal contents, with the proviso that the archetypes which rule in the total psychological make-up are decided by the specific configuration of the planets at birth. The planets which are symbolic of psychic drives will be discussed in Chapter 7.

The Houses
The psychic structure of a man has been mentioned several times already. This structure is closely bound up with the division of the horoscope into twelve sectors known as the houses of the horoscope. The houses are traditionally taken to represent the circumstances and situations which will enter into the life of the individual. Modern psychological opinion has advanced the viewpoint that there is a significant relationship between events outside the individual and his psychological make-up. Now, the houses as indicators of circumstances are also the representatives of areas in the human psyche; a point to which we shall return in Chapter VI.

The meaning contained in the houses is analogous to the meaning of the zodiac signs. Thus, the first house indicates circumstances which are analogous to the characteristics of Aries, the second house corresponds to Taurus, etc. Each house has a starting-point and and end-point, and where one house ends the next one begins. The starting-point of a given house is termed the cusp of that house. An astrologer might say, when speaking of a certain horoscope, that the 'second cusp is in Leo', meaning that the starting-point of the second house is the sign of Leo. There are, accordingly, twelve house cusps, some of which are so important that they have been given special names:

The Ascendant	cusp of first house
The Descendant	cusp of seventh house
The M.C. (Medium Coeli or Midheaven)	cusp of tenth house
The I.C. (Imum Coeli or Lower Heaven)	cusp of fourth house

The Aspects

As seen from the earth (the horoscope is geocentric of course), one planet appears in one direction and another planet appears in the same or in some other direction. Except when they coincide, they are observed to make a certain angle with one another. When the angle is of a certain size, the planets concerned are said to form an aspect. Aspects are formed by angles when 360° (the number of degrees in a complete circle) is divided by a whole number (1, 2, 3, 4, 5, 6, 7, 8, 9, 10, 20). Multiples of the angles produced in this way (2x, 3x or 5x) may also count as aspects. At the same time, a distinction is made between major and minor aspects. The major ones have the more obvious effects; so much so that very many astrological books limit themselves to these. It seems however, that in practice, the minor aspects are by no means negligible.

The admissible deviation in degrees from the exact degree of formation of an aspect is called an orb. In general the orb allowed for major aspects is greater than that allowed for minor aspects. In other words, a major aspect will still 'work' with a measure of inaccuracy where the influence of a minor aspect would become insignificant.

The aspects indicate the way in which given psychic contents are in general integrated. Two planets, analogous to two different factors in our psyche, make contact through a minor or major aspect and then the shared significance of the aspect in question decides the way in which the contact between the psychic factors works out. Difficult aspects such as the square and opposition demand from an individual more effort and application on his part to develop as a harmonious and balanced person than do the traditionally styled 'favourable' aspects such as the trine and sextile. Nevertheless, the aspects with more tension in them also contain the energy required to release that tension or, as they case may be, to integrate the psychic factors concerned into the whole psyche.

The upshot is that we cannot talk about 'good' or 'bad' aspects and leave it at that. The very tension and resistance evoked inwardly and/or outwardly by each so-called 'bad' aspect thrusts it into conscious recognition and can, therefore, lead a person to a greater insight into his own psychic structure and help him to be more cautious in his indulgence in certain idiosyncrasies. This opportunity for development is what we may call their good side. A difficult aspect need not always bring problems; its creative opportunities are equally available. On the other hand 'good' aspects will become lost opportunities for lack of stimulus. With few tensions, a person may fail to realize his full potential and what could be so easily attained goes by the board. Therefore the traditional meanings of the aspects must be taken in conjunction with their opposites. As Elisabeth Haich once remarked: 'There are no bad energies, only energies which are badly used.'

The Major Aspects

Name	Symbol	Size in degrees	Orb
Conjunction	☌	0	6 to 8
Sextile	✳	60	4 to 6
Square	☐	90	6 to 8
Trine	△	120	6 to 8
Quincunx or Inconjunct*	⚼	150	3
Opposition	☍	180	6 to 9

Fig. 2.8

Minor Aspects

Name	Symbol	Size in degrees	Orb
Vigintile	人	18	1 to 2
Semi-sextile	⋁	30	2
Semi-quintile or Decile	⊥	36	2
Novile	N	40	2
Semi-square	L	45	2
Septile	S	51° 25′ 34″	1
Quintile*	Q	72	2
Tridecile	¥ T	108	2
Sesquiquadrate	⊿	135	2
Biquintile*	BQ	144	2

*There is some disagreement as to whether these aspects should be regarded as major or minor. Also, there is no complete unanimity on the symbols to be used for the minor aspects; probably because they are employed by many fewer astrologers than employ and agree on the symbols for the major aspects.

Fig. 2.9

Rulers

Each sign has a planet with which it has a special relationship and the sign gives optimum scope to the characteristics of the planet concerned. This applies both to its constructive and to its destructive characteristics.

The planet is called the ruler of the particular sign. Some signs have two rulers allocated to them. This happened after the

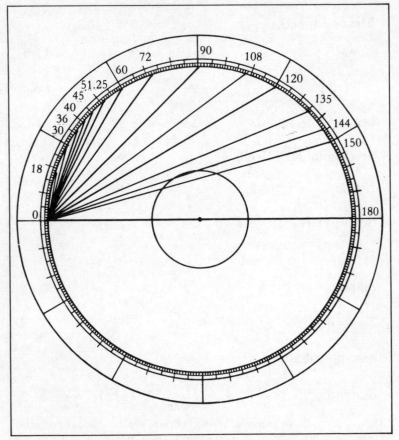

Fig. 2.10 Aspects in a Horoscope Chart

discovery of Uranus in 1781, Neptune in 1846 and Pluto in 1930. Before Uranus was discovered, occidental astrologers worked with the known planets, Mercury, Venus, Mars, Jupiter and Saturn plus the sun and moon (Hindu astrology had for a long time used undiscovered planets). Each of the original planets ruled two signs, and the sun and moon ruled one each. Subsequent to the discovery of Uranus, Neptune and Pluto, this system underwent a certain amount of change. Complete agreement has not yet been reached on the rulership of Pluto, but most astrologers see it as the ruler of Scorpio.

The rulerships are given in Fig. 2.10. The day rulers are usually considered to exercise their influence over the

Sign	Symbol	Day ruler	Night ruler
Aries	♈	♂ Mars	⯓ Pluto
Taurus	♉	♀ Venus	
Gemini	♊	☿ Mercury	
Cancer	♋	☽ Moon	
Leo	♌	☉ Sun	
Virgo	♍	☿ Mercury	
Libra	♎	♀ Venus	
Scorpio	♏	⯓ Pluto	♂ Mars
Sagittarius	♐	♃ Jupiter	♆ Neptune
Capricorn	♑	♄ Saturn	⛢ Uranus
Aquarius	♒	⛢ Uranus	♄ Saturn
Pisces	♓	♆ Neptune	♃ Jupiter

Fig. 2.11 Signs and Rulers

conscious part of the sign in question while the night ruler governs the unconscious part. The absence of a number of night rulers has led some astrologers to postulate the existence of undiscovered planets such as were assumed long ago by Hindu astrology.*

No attempt has been made to provide a complete exposition in this chapter. It has only been possible to mention some of the leading astrological elements by way of introduction to the following chapters, where many of the factors broached here will be further discussed and elucidated.

*It should perhaps be pointed out that the details of day and night rulerships given in Fig. 2.11 are not in complete agreement with the traditional rulerships. The sun should rule the day in Leo and the moon the night in Cancer. The other planets each have day and night houses. E.g. Mercury's day house is Gemini and its night house is Virgo.

Translator's note.

3

The Quadruplicities as Forms of Psychic Energy

Energy

It makes little difference whether we examine the processes of nature, explore old philosophies of life, study astrology or try to gain insight in some other way, we always encounter a number of fundamental laws of life. In the present case the chief law is that nothing remains in its original state. Heraclitus formulated this long ago under the name *enantiodromia*, which means, roughly speaking, that everything eventually turns into its opposite. On that score, Jung stated that all things human are relative, because everything rests on inner antitheses which are forms of energy. 'Energy necessarily rests on a pre-existing contrast without which no energy would be possible .... First we must have high and low, hot and cold etc. before that process of adjustment known as energy can take place. All life is energy and therefore rests on opposition. The aim is not to convert one value into its opposite but to maintain both values as they are while recognizing the contrast between them.'

The importance of the principle of opposites has already been indicated in Chapter 2, and we have already touched on the fact that things are only recognizable as good and bad by contrasting one with the other. If there were no 'bad', it would be impossible to appreciate 'good' for there would be no opportunity to make any comparison between the two. 'For only by the intensity of the darkness can the rays of light become visible in all their intensity. Light and dark compose a day and good and evil make a person human.' Jung also says, quite correctly, that when someone shows people his dark side, they know he must have a light side, and he who is aware at the same time of both his dark and his light side sees himself from two angles from middle ground. He realizes that dark and light go to make up the world. If one identifies with only one of the two opposites, either the good or the bad, the quality one does not want to be identified with is evoked just as strongly – if not in the conscious mind then in the unconscious. Whenever an individual makes up his mind to be nothing but good, his approach becomes one-sided. There is nothing wrong with 'goodness' in itself, of course, but by clamping down consciously on his behaviour he arouses an unconscious force – the evil he refuses to acknowledge – and this, as is usual in such cases of repression, works to compensate or even undermine the consciously-chosen but one-sided habit. Every form of addiction, whether it be to alcohol, morphine or idealism, provokes a reaction eventually. Good and evil form a paradoxical whole. The recognition of both opposites makes the concepts good and evil relative and this relativity is applicable to *every* part of life. Everything has two sides and both opposites are present at one and the same time, although *one* side shows itself most clearly and so becomes noticed.

The human psyche (which is composed of the opposites, 'conscious' and 'unconscious') strives, like everything else in nature, to attain a balance and so it is completely natural that a big action in one part of the psyche produces an equal and opposite reaction in the other part of the psyche. Thus, for example, great positive intellectual feats in consciousness are often followed by strong emotional reactions of a negative character. The idea of *enantiodromia* – the fact that everything changes into its opposite or reverse side – finds expression in our lives as in the example just given. Both aspects of a single reality continually alternate. 'Thus, in the natural course of events, positive effects follow negative ones in the unconscious and *vice versa*. If our fantasy produces a bright image at one moment, there is a dark one to follow immediately afterwards. It falls to the lot of our *psychic energy* to ensure the mutual regulation of these relationships and to preserve them in a state of living tension. For all these pairs of opposites are to be thought of as opposed not only in content but also in the intensity of their energies.'

On relating this to the saying from the Tao Teh King which heads Chapter 2, we see that the whole principle is laid down in the words 'Two brings forth three'. The structure of the opposites (Two) necessarily calls a third factor (Three) into play, i.e. the energy these two opposites strive to reunite. It is this (psychic) energy which is indicated in astrology by the concept of the quadruplicity and the three quadruplicities illustrate three different directions of flow of this complex energy unit.

Heraclitus and Carl Jung are not the only authorities who have spoken of the principle of opposites; the idea is prominent in many forms in many cultures. A splendid example is to be found in ancient Chinese thought, as presented to the West by Richard Wilhelm, where the attempt is made to bridge over the two (apparently irreconcilable) antipoles on the assumptions that opposites eventually meet. It is thought that two conditions, however antagonistic, become compatible by succeeding one another in the course of time in such a way that the one turns into the other. This is in fact the basic idea of the I Ching, The Book of Changes. Time is the key to opposition and reconciliation.

The Cycle of Events

The I Ching shows that the Chinese realized long ago that everything is subject to change and is, after the passage of time, converted into its opposite. On studying this rhythm, we notice that there are four seasons of three months each. The first months holds the promise of the whole season and ushers it in; the second months forms the climax of the season and gives prominence to the initial impulse for a certain steady period. Then comes the inevitable third month, with its gradual preparation for the change-over to the next season. Enshrined within it is the idea of releasing the old to make way for the new. The end of a season is already present in its beginning; just as birth inevitably implies death at some later date. The fact that it is summer tells us that winter is on its way and *vice versa*.

Within the rhythmic changes of the seasons there is another rhythm for our consideration; that is to say the beginning, the middle and the end or rather the first, second and final months. The cardinal sign is the sign in which a new season is given the definitive form that is maintained in the fixed sign for a while. The mutable sign closes the season by dissolving and diffusing the old so that the new season can take its place.

The current of life energy that we experience in the rhythm of the seasons is anchored, from an astrological point of view, in the principle of the quadruplicities. The universal rhythm of becoming, being and passing away, mirrored in the seasonal cycle and in the three quadruplicities of astrology, also lies at the basis of the pattern in The Book of Changes. An insight into this pattern can greatly strengthen our understanding of the quadruplicities; which is reason enough, it seems to me, to look at it in greater detail.

The I Ching, or Book of Changes, consists of 64 hexagrams with an explanatory commentary on each. A hexagram is composed of six lines and falls into two trigrams of three lines each. The meaning of the words 'hexagram' as 'six-fold diagram' and 'trigram' as 'three-fold diagram' are self-explanatory. Altogether, there are eight different trigrams. These trigrams are themselves made up of broken and/or unbroken lines. 'In the world of polar opposites, the primary, positive pole is represented by an unbroken (Yang) line and the secondary, negative pole by a broken (Yin) line'

———   Yang, unbroken, positive, the principle of light.

— —   Yin, broken, negative, the principle of darkness.

'And so associated with the original state, a triunity lies at the basis of reality. In the words of Lao Tse, "The One assimilates the Two, the Two assimilates the Three and the Three assimilates All Things." This is the received doctrine on the origin of all phenomena.'

The above quotations from Richard Wilhelm point to the fact that through the duality (the Two) of terrestrial existence and by means of the flow of (psychic) energy, man can return to the centre. This is the starting point (or 'original state', as Wilhelm terms it) preceding manifestation by duality.

The two opposites plus the uniting equilibrating energy are therefore a trinity forming the foundation of reality. This three-in-oneness is symbolized in the I Ching by the trigram. Three lines, any of which may be either broken or unbroken, allow a possible combination of $2^2 = 8$. These eight trigrams represent the combination of the masculine, unbroken line in its threefold mode of occurrence with the feminine, broken line in·a similar three-fold mode. The possible variations are as follows:

☰	K'IEN,*	the Creative One, the father
☷	KW'UN,	the Receptive One, the mother
☳	CHAN	the Quickening One, the eldest son
☵	K'AN	the Unfathomable One, the second son
☶	KAN	the Solitary One, the youngest son
☴	SUN	the Amenable One, the eldest daughter
☲	LI	the Shining or Clinging One, the second daughter
☱	T'UI	the Joyful One, the youngest daughter.

The first trigram, the Creative One, is the opposite of the second, the Receptive One. It imparts a progressive movement. There is no going back for the Creative One; it has an opening type of movement and its psychological counterpart is what Jung called extroversion. The Receptive One appears to be at rest. It retains its movement within itself and is shut up; therefore it clearly corresponds to the concept of introversion (for further information on these concepts see Chapter 4). This dichotomy is also comparable with the astrological subdivision into positive and negative signs.

Ancient Chinese thought expressed itself pictorially and, as a result of this mode of thinking, the entire I Ching has been written in a sort of symbolism, so that the book is not easily accessible to Westerners like ourselves who think in much more abstract terms. Thus, the first trigram, the Creative One, is called the father and the trigram of the Receptive One is called the mother. These two trigrams, pictorially represented as father and mother, express the principle of polar opposites, which Western minds would probably prefer to define as positive and negative. From the abstract point of view, there is a flow of energy between the positive and negative poles. Chinese thought sees this as the union of father and mother, resulting in the birth of children after the energy flow. Of the eight basic trigrams, these two symbolize the parents while the remaining six are the children: three daughters and three sons.

*The spellings are taken from Creative Energy by I. and L.E. Mears. John Murray, 1931.

A wealth of wisdom lies concealed within this collection of images. The positive-negative (or masculine-feminine, light-dark, etc.) polarity, as we have already named it , can reveal itself in three ways analogous to the three quadruplicities and to the three months in a season. Pictured as a family tree, we have the man and wife polarity worked out to its logical conclusion in the two times three children, each sex having three representatives, i.e. the eldest, second and youngest son or daughter as they case may be. On further investigation, we see that, from the psychological angle, the masculine-feminine polarity goes even further because, on the evidence of the lines of their trigrams, the males had an unconscious female component and the females an unconscious male component.

The principles underlying the order of the images of the eldest, second and youngest son or daughter are the same as those underlying the rhythm of the seasons and the order of the quadruplicities: cardinal, fixed and mutable.

The eldest son, Chăn, is described as etheric energy, the Quickening One, and is symbolized by the electricity which stirs in the earth in early spring. The eldest daughter, Sun, is symbolized by the wind, that finds its way into everything without force and so is ubiquitous. It is the principle of penetration; not a percussive type of penetration, like its male counterpart, but more passive. The starting impulse symbolized here is the same as that with which the seasons begin in their first months. The cardinal cross is analogous and, although very diverse descriptions of the quadruplicities are supplied in the various astrology books, the writers agree on the activity, the creativity, the industry and the idea of making a beginning found in the cardinal signs, Aries, Cancer, Libra and Capricorn.

The second son, K'an, is symbolized by the energy that has been delegated to water; the energy of the movement within itself. It takes the form of water, rain, waterfall, cloud etc. The second daughter, Li, is the flame; the flame that attaches itself and needs something other than itself, something combustible, before it can make its appearance. Whenever it can fasten on to something and rest on it, then it can give light and visibility. The different forms adopted by water and the burning of fire are processes which take their rise from something outside them; something else necessarily precedes them. Water *remains* water, however, and fire *remains* fire. There is no change. And, what is more, immutability is also a characteristic of the fixed cross, along with fixity, inertia, stability and perseveration. The members of the fixed cross are Taurus, Leo, Scorpio and Aquarius.

The youngest son, K'an, has the mountain as a symbol. In ancient China, the mountain had a significance different from that attributed to it in the West. The mountain was regarded as a centre of life and was not seen isolated from its surroundings. The idea of a mountain included everything living and growing on it, not forgetting the clouds it produced. Richard Wilhelm has this to say about it: '... because the heavenly is, so to speak, focused here on the earth – the earth lies below and the sky arches overhead – atmospheric influences are drawn down and life attains a state of harmony.' T'ui, the youngest daughter, is equally in harmony and, like the mountain, encompasses life and death. T'ui is the autumn, a joyful time of harvest but also the time when nature begins to die: 'that golden jollity conceals a relentless harshness; not yet apparent perhaps, but already there within.' T'ui is symbolized by water in the form of a tranquil lake and is therefore distinguished from the various (spontaneously moving) forms of K'an, the second son. The close of one season and the preparation for the next is summed up within this ripening and decay. The preceding quadruplicities find not only their harmony but also their resolution in the mutable cross which is the astrological counterpart of the youngest son and the youngest daughter. In addition, the mutable cross brings change, modification, reduced stability and a certain type of obsequiousness. Harmony is also ascribed to this cross. After this movement towards balance and harmony and after this process of fading and dissolution, a new beginning is possible and we return to the cardinal signs once more. The signs of Gemini, Virgo, Sagittarius and Pisces belong to the mutable (and final) quadruplicity.

Through all the above, shines the simple truth already mentioned: nothing remains in its original form. Life is a continuous change from commencement and growth, through stabilization and maturity to a search for harmony and final dissolution, making way for renewed growth. This concept of energy is pictorially represented in the construction of the I Ching and is found in nature in the rhythm of the seasons and also in astrology in the principle of the quadruplicities. Further in Jungian psychology, it is bound up with the idea of the libido (not to be confused with the limited libido concept of Freud), psychic energy or life force.

Life Force

Just as the whole of nature and the whole of life is one great movement, so the psychic system of man, as an integral part of nature and life, is in constant movement. Carl Jung considers its cause to be the psychic force and this he defines as '... the total force flowing through and linking with one another all the forms and activities of this psychic system'. Psychic energy or libido is the intensity of the psychic process and its psychological value. In his book, *Psychological Types*, Jung suggests further that 'psychological value' is not another term for matter-of-fact, aesthetic or intellectual value judgement; the 'value' is rather given by the determinative force which finds expression in certain psychic activities or achievements. In fact, the concept 'psychic energy' has nothing to do with the existence or otherwise of psychic power, it is a form of energy in the sense known to physics. This energy is characterized by the fact that it is not present 'in person' so to speak in the world of objective phenomena but is only given in our own, subjective experience. Jolande Jacobi, in his *The Psychology of C.G. Jung*, clarifies this statement as follows: 'In everyday circumstances, the psychic energy is always manifested in the specific phenomena of the psyche, such as drives, wishes, decisions, affects, work output etc. The will, for example, is a special case of consciously directed psychic energy. However, when the psychic energy is only potentially present, it makes itself felt as particular skills, possibilites, attitudes etc.'

Carl Jung concludes that the psychic process is a living process and in this respect he regards the psychic energy or libido as a 'particularization' of the life energy with a specific function to fulfil; that is to say it has to preserve a mutual balance between the opposites while keeping them under constant tension. The greater the opposition in a certain psychic process, the more intensely will the psychic energy manifest itself in the form of actions, mental images, dreams etc. This is because the psyche is a self-regulating system and always strives to preserve a balance by releasing the flow of psychic energy or libido. There is certainly no need for this transference of the libido to be a conscious process; on the contrary, we see that unconscious processes are called into play by means of the libido whenever the conscious processes have led to a position in which the psyche of the individual has become too unbalanced.

It appears from the foregoing that the libido can suffer transference, and this is in full agreement with the laws of physics; e.g. when something 'falls', there is a flow of energy. Carl Jung expressly states that the quantity of energy in a psychic system remains constant, only its distribution is variable. In the case of opposites in the psyche, a concentration of energy in one pole will automatically lead to the withdrawal of energy from the opposite pole. This can continue until the imbalance is too great; the effect is a reverse flow of energy.

Carl Jung makes a clear distinction between the directions in which psychic energy moves. The progressive movement is fundamentally different from the regressive, but both are indispensable in our daily life. They must not be confused with such concepts as good and bad nor with those of evolution and involution, since no value judgements can be passed on these indications of energy movements. They are much more like a diastole and systole, where the diastole would be an extrovert expansion of the libido into the universe and the systole its contraction into the individual. Jung went on to say that the progressive movement took its direction from the consciousness. He remarked, 'it consists of a continuous and unhampered process of adjustment to conscious requirements imposed by life, and of the differentiation of adaptation and function type thus entailed.' (See Chapter 4 for the latter ideas.) Dr Gerhard Adler writes:

In order to achieve this (adjustment), the individual is nearly always inclined to become one-sided, because he is compelled to take account of practical realities. Whoever is accustomed to tackling practical problems by means of rational thought, does not find it easy to allow equal scope to his feelings; so, when placed in a situation from which he is unable to extricate himself by thinking it through, he is helpless. One could say that his libido is like a big river full of pack-ice choking the shipping lanes; its free flow is blocked. Whereas it is essential to this free flow that impulses and their counter-impulses should annul and efface one another – as, for instance, in the process of weighing arguments for and against something – a blockage is characterized by a conflict which creates such internal tension that an effort is made at repression. This, however, prepares the way for a neurosis. The actions arising out of a situation of this type are resisted by the disturbing influence of the repressed counter-impulses. The influence is a disturbing one because repressed impulses exercise an effect opposite to that of conscious tendencies, as is only to be expected from the very nature of the case. Now, as soon as the conflict commences, there is a simultaneous reverse flow of the libido preparing the way for a resolution of the difficulty on another level. This is the process known as regression in which the lost intensity of flow is again evident. And here is where it becomes practically impossible to contain those forces of which no notice is taken in practice and therefore are seldom or never used; in other words the forces of the unconscious.

Now, while Freud would trace these forces to their causes, treating them as repressions which have created the neurotic conflict, without recognizing any usefulness they may have for the psyche, and while Alfred Adler seeks to reduce these unconscious factors and nullify their effect, Jung sees a highly constructive value in them. That is to say, they hold within them the necessary adaptation function (for the given situation) which has not taken shape so far but is expressed for the time being in embryonic or archaic and undeveloped form. (N.B. This archaic and undeveloped form has given rise to the erroneous opinion that we are dealing with nothing but primitive values here, whereas in fact it is the nature of the unconscious itself which imposes an archaic form of expression). Thus in this respect, regression, by activating the contents of the unconscious, has the means for another kind of free flow and makes possible an improved adaptation. Seen in this light, regression represents a falling back on the inexhaustible power reserves of the unconscious and their as yet unapparent possibilities.

It would seem from this excellent analysis that, in a regression, the unconscious is intensified willy-nilly and may even become overcharged with energy, giving rise to unintended or unconscious reactions. So we should certainly not treat it as negative; it is merely a mechanism in the psyche for tackling a failure and eventually restoring the psychic equilibrium. What is more, after the complexes which have been brought to the surface have been assimilated, the psychic channel is left open wider than before.

Everyday life goes hand-in-hand with alternate progressive and regressive processes. Everything we consciously desire or do, every perception and every psychic effort, are all forms of the progressive flow of the libido. On the other hand, fatigue, absent-mindedness, sleep and emotional reactions are manifestations of the regressive flow of the libido, so necessary to ensure that the progressive flow does not become unbalanced or, if it does, to ensure that its equilibrium is restored. In short, we can say that the progressive flow is based on the need for adjustment to the outside world and that the regressive flow is based on the need for internal adjustment, i.e. to the inner 'law' of the individual. Progression and regression are simply phases in the circulation of energy, by means of which the intensity of the flow is determined by the difference in loading between the various psychological factors.

The Quadruplicities as Directions taken by the Life Force

When we take a look at the progressive flow of the libido in the light of the quadruplicities, there is little doubt where the cardinal cross fits in. It symbolizes the outgoing, driving force in the universe plus movement and energy. Its movement is a forward one and its power is creative; hence it adjusts to the world outside. C. Aq. Libra describes the relationship between the cardinal cross and consciousness as the desire to manifest, and it is worth noting in this connection that Olga von Ungern-Sternberg characterized the cardinal cross as the basic structure of the image of man and as a creative and manifesting idea.

The regressive flow of the libido in adjustment to the inner world is found in the fixed cross; to which C. Aq. Libra ascribes fixation-solidification. R.C. Jansky comments that those who are strongly influenced by the fixed cross are inclined to look for everything they need within and not outside themselves. Von Ungern-Sternberg calls the fixed cross the cross of fate. It is symbolized by the Sphinx, which embodies the riddle of life. The Bull (Taurus) forms its body, the Lion (Leo) its limbs armed with claws, the Scorpion (Scorpio) gives it its wings (because the Eagle is the symbol of the transformed Scorpion) and the Water-bearer (Aquarius) gives it its head. Those it influences are in a state of being locked up within themselves and this is also the case with the second month in a season and the second son and daughter of the I Ching system of trigrams.

In the third quadruplicity, or mutable cross, we see the two previous crosses united: 'wisdom and harmony crystallize out of the two preceding forces.' says C. Aq. Libra, and that means that both the regressive and the progressive energy flow are contained in this cross. That is why the mutable cross has always been seen as diffusive or movable. It is the quadruplicity where preparations are made for the new, and in which the regressive movement is converted into the progressive one. The regressive flow promotes the germination of a new psychological health; a general adjustment becomes possible, and the flow can once again become progressive. It was named the Calvary Cross by Olga von Ungern-Sternberg, and she finds agreement in the words of M.E. Hone that each sign composing this cross has its own special way of expressing mutability and contains the wish to serve. The energy which included both progression *and* regression is in keeping with the image of the youngest son and youngest daughter in the I Ching, i.e. decay and growth, death and life – two different direction of energy-flow, with the accent on preparation for the next phase.

Heinrich Kündig, credits the cardinal cross with a great intensity which can stem from the progressive movement of the libido. This is outgoing and is felt strongly in the external world and, certainly more strongly than the regressive movement is felt. He then assigns a moderate intensity to the fixed cross. He finds that the mutable cross has a weak intensity, possibly because at one time it is progressive and at another regressive, which makes it seem rather superficial and aimless. The energy flow in the mutable cross, however, is the least clear of any to the observer owing to its dualistic character. It adapts, integrates and resolves at one and the same time.

Coming back to the Tao Teh King, quoted at the beginning

of Chapter 2, we see that while the whole of life is split up into apparent opposites, both in our psyche and in the outside world, these opposites do, however, strive after harmony with one another. Psychic energy or libido arises from this duality as a third factor in order to create a balance. This it can do in three different ways, which express themselves in the cycle of all natural events. First there is coming into existence; second, continuance and culmination; and third, disintegration. These processes are enshrined in ancient books of wisdom like the Tao Teh King and I Ching, as well as in the astrological tradition. Modern psychology, too, recognizes the same energy cycle.

Each quadruplicity comprises two positive and two negative signs. So the energy within a quadruplicity has a more extrovert action on two occasions and a more introvert one on the remaining two occasions. Here is the explanation of the apparent anomaly that the rather retiring Crab (Cancer) is one of the signs in the creative and active Cardinal cross. Although, in principle, the Crab is fairly introvert, it functions very well as the driving and sustaining force behind a partner, helping in the achievement of his or her personal ambitions. The principle of the energy contained in the quadruplicities should not be given a material interpretation but should be regarded as something present in the psyche and in nature *before* any concrete form is assumed.

Psychic energy serves to resolve or control tensions and inner conflicts. The gist of this fundamental idea is contained in the name and construction of that astrological concept, the quadruplicity. The latter has an inner tension due to the fact that it is made up of two pairs of opposing signs and of four elements mutually exclusive in content. And so, in the quadruplicities, we have what may be described as an internal tension; they are triunities composed of four parts (four signs). The elements, on the other hand, display external tension but have an internal harmony. The four elements each consist of three signs similar in character; they are four sets of three.

'Two brings forth three and three brings forth the ten thousand things' can be taken to mean that where we have the system of two opposites plus their equilibrating third factor (the libido), they can enter matter under endless guises. On earth, this expression of the diversity of life occurs in various ways, although their infinite variety may be traced back to the number four, for which we have the astrological symbols: fire, earth, air and water.

4

The Four Elements and
Psychological Types

The Quaternity
An age-old symbolic meaning lies hidden in the number four;
a meaning which can be traced back to the earliest cultures. In
our material world we constantly encounter expressions in
which it plays an important part: the four points of the
compass, the four seasons, the four quarters of the moon etc.
In more spiritual matters, we have the four castes of India, the
four ways of spiritual development in Buddhism and the four
Evangelists. For the alchemists, the number four, or the
principle of the quaternity, was a basis and a point of departure
for preparing the 'Stone of the Wise'.

Carl Jung counts the quaternity as an archetype and says:

> ... it is the logical condition for every general judgement. Anyone
> who tries to form a judgement of this type will find that it must have
> a fourfold aspect. For example, anyone who wants to describe the
> totality of the horizon, names the four points of the compass. The
> ideal totality is the circle, but its natural minimum division is a
> division into four.

On comparing this dictum of Jung's with how the idea of the
quaternity is rendered in Tibetan Buddhism, we see that the
so-called Stupa (a symbol for the structure of creation in its
entirety) is made up of five layers, representing the five
elements: earth, fire, water, air and ether. The element ether
is somewhat different from the others, forming as it were the
source *and* destination of the other four elements which are
used in the West. Thus the element ether is comparable with
Jung's 'circle' or, psychologically speaking, with the 'Self'; the
totality out of which everything issues and to which everything
returns. Of which, indeed, the elements fire, earth, air and

water are the expression in the sense that they are the four states in which matter can show itself on earth: earth being the equivalent of the solid state, water of the liquid state, air of the gaseous state and fire of plasma.

The circle, the element ether, the Self, the Philosophers' Stone etc., all signify the same thing and are expressed in astrology in the chart of the horoscope as a whole. Nowadays it is printed in the shape of a circle but formerly it was drawn as a square!

The four elements may be regarded as the corner-stone of astrology; they are essential components of the astrological description of man. Quite early on, the attempt was made to divide human beings into four groups, and the system that appears to have become most widely known is that of the temperaments: the choleric, the melancholic, sanguine and phlegmatic. These correspond to the colour types: red, blue, yellow and green, and they in turn agree with the astrological elements: fire, earth, air and water. The whole thing has now been updated and given a psychological perspective by Carl Jung in his four psychological functions: intuition, perception, thinking and feeling.

A psychological function is a certain psychic form of activity which remains fundamentally unchanged in differing circumstances or, to put it more simply, the psychological function represents an essential mental attitude. Each of us can orientate ourselves in one of the following four ways:

- we can perceive; that is to say we can ascertain the presence of something. Reliance is placed on individual observations made via the senses;   (SENSATION)

- we can think; meaning we can determine what it is that we have perceived with a view to fitting it into our own (mental) picture of reality; (INTELLECT)

- we can feel: which means we can take note of the feelings of pleasure of distaste evoked by something and use them to decide whether to accept or reject it; (FEELING)

- we can rely on intuition; or in other words can 'know' in some irrational fashion where a thing has come from
(INTUITION)

and/or where it will lead to. This is, so to speak, to look behind its external appearance.

The form of intuition intended here is not what is usually called Uranian intuition by astrologers. The latter consists of flashes of recognition and the relationship between this recognition and material entities is completely normal. The psychological function termed intuition is much more a conscious approach to everyday life in which the individual immerses himself without reflection in the stream of events and lets himself go with it.

These psychological functions produce two polarities. On the one hand, there are the rational pair, thinking and feeling. They are called rational because they are appreciative and concerned with value judgements. Thinking differentiates truth from error and feeling distinguishes between what is attractive and what is unattractive. On the other hand, there are the two so-called irrational functions: perception and intuition. They are termed irrational because no judgement is attached to their observations. Perception accepts material data at their face value, while intuition acts more with what Jolande Jacobi calls 'inner perception', or seeing the possibilities in things.

Then again, two further polarities are contained within this division: i.e. thinking versus feeling and perception versus intuition. None of these functions exhibit a connection with the others nor can they be converted into one another. And so, Carl Jung, after years of practice and a lifetime of empirical research, gradually worked out this division into four which bears the following analogy to the four astrological elements:

- the element fire corresponds to the intuitive function:
- the element earth to the function of perception;
- the element air to the thinking function;
- the element water to the feeling function.

Perception and intuition, as irrational functions, are characteristic of the psychological behaviour of the child and of so-called primitives. Intuition makes it possible for the child and for primitive man to see mythological images (the precursors of ideas) behind their obtrusive sense impressions.

It supplements perception and is also the rich source out of which thinking and feeling arise as rational (i.e. appraising) functions. The succession of fire and earth followed by air and water as elements in astrology fits in well with this arrangement when we take them in order from the beginning, starting with the fire sign Aries. It should not be concluded, however, that the elements fire and earth are in any way inferior to those of air and water; it is just that their action is different. Each one of us has all four elements in the circle of his horoscope chart, and all four are necessary for a balanced development of the personality.

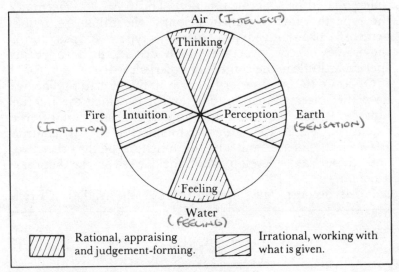

Fig. 4.1 The Elements and the Human Psyche.

The Four Functions in the Human Psyche

Man is disposed to exercise all four of these functions and they enable him to orientate himself in the here and now just as efficiently as length and breadth enable him to find his bearings in the geographical sense. Experience, however, has taught him that it is always on the basis of only one of these functions that he adjusts to reality. In the development of this one function, the individual's constitution plays an important though not always a decisive role. In families, for instance, we sometimes see at a quite early stage an apparent distribution of functions. One member is the introvert, another is the young man, a third is the thinker etc. The others do not hesitate in leaving certain functions to the members of the family who are more at home with them. This all happens unconsciously in a period when the main function is in the process of crystallization. This main function develops and becomes differentiated with increasing strength and the individual learns to use the function consciously with increasing assurance as an act of will, although the initial 'choice' of this main function is an unconscious process in most instances. Because it develops more vigorously and quickly than the other three functions, the main function is also named the differentiated or superior function. This function determines the type to which a person belongs: the thinking, feeling, perceptive or intuitive type. A person's type so to speak forms the framework or structure which decides in advance his specific attitude to the content of experience.

Opposite to the superior function in the human psyche, we have the inferior function. The extent to which the inferior function is unreliable and unconscious is proportional to the extent to which the superior function is under control. Between the inferior and superior functions lie the other two, and these can develop into ancillaries of the superior function.

It has become clear, mainly through the studies of Erich

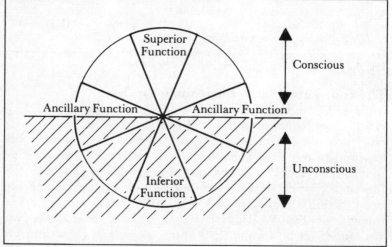

Fig. 4.2 The Four Functions

Nuemann, (See *The Origins and History of Consciousness*) that the unconscious is the starting-point both in the development of the human race and in that of the child.

Consciousness develops little by little out of this unconscious state as a result of all kinds of experience. Originally it is formless and like an island floating on the ocean of the unknown, but later it takes a more settled form. The totality of the personality lies concealed within the unconscious psyche and all four functions are present in it. As already said, these functions begin to crystallize due to certain disposition and a growing number of experiences. Quite quickly a single function predominates and has the best opportunity of developing into the superior function, i.e. that function which is utilized by the ego in order to organize the field of conciousness. The conscious mind can also gain control over a second, and later on, a third function, but the inferior function remains the property of the unconscious. In practice, our theoretical model amounts to this, that in addition to exercising the main function by which he has been 'type-cast', the individual also makes use of a second comparatively differentiated ancillary function. For most of us, it is only seldom that the third function comes within reach; the fourth, or inferior, function is entirely out of the control of the will.

From an astrological point of view, all this means that eventually one element (together with any sensitive points positioned in it, such as the planets) attains total development and becomes the basis for the overall view of the subject's life and general behaviour pattern. According to this theory of function-type the element opposite the superior element, will manifest as the inferior function with all the characteristics of the lattter. Owing to the strong connection the inferior function has with the unconscious, it is inert, unreliable, open to influence and uncertain in use. Its ways of expressing itself often display a childlike, archaic, passionately primitive and often compulsive character. Here is one of the reasons why capricious and whimsical behaviour is sometimes seen in those of whom we would least expect it – the inferior function has gained the upper hand for the time being.

Because of the incompatability of the two contrasting psychological functions, it is impossible for them to appear simultaneously or to be equally fully-fledged. It should, however, be pointed out, to avoid any misunderstanding, that the antagonism of functions has nothing to do with astrological oppositions. In the oppositions we have a single theme that is taken up from two different angles. The signs in opposition, Cancer and Capricorn for example, have form as a common theme; Cancer symbolizes fluid and Capricorn fixed form. Whereas their modes or expressing the separate theme are in contrast, their point of departure is the same. In the four psychological functions, on the other hand, the points of departure are always totally different and therefore irreconcilable.

Thus, in astrology, the elements air and water make *no* opposition with one another (nor do fire and earth), and this is reason enough why they have very little in common. Any conflict between these elements, as for instance between air and water, corresponds to some conflict between thinking and feeling. When, for example, the element air, or the function of thinking, predominates in consciousness, the problem arises that events which are best assimilated via the feelings (or element water) are first approached by thinking, so that the feelings themselves have little opportunity for development. It is true, of course, that in such case one can try to reason the events out and approach them more emotionally later, but the supremacy of thinking becomes apparent when, as in the example, we treat air as a superior element. However, the feeling function comes to the front or, to put it another way, if the water element is emphasized, we observe the straight-forward thinker in an especially sentimental and over-sensitive mood. His state of mind is outside his own control since the inferior function, as already mentioned, is not ruled by the will.

The fact that the superior function always prevails in a certain way over the inferior function appears from the many efforts made by the human consciousness to channel and organize all the uncontrolled actions and reactions of the inferior function. The tenor of the simplest expression of the inferior function can be so changed as eventually to fit in with the subject-matter of the superior function. Marie-Louise of France gives a fine example of this in her description of the intuitive type who attempts to use his inferior perceptive function. This situation may fairly be interpreted as the astrological fire type trying to utilize the earth component in his horoscope. Thus, at a certain moment, someone may feel drawn to the idea of sculpting or modelling. These things help the suppressed perceptive function (earth) of the intuitive person (fire) to rise nearer the surface, because he makes close contact with concrete materials of one sort or another. He may make something out of lump of clay, for example an ill-shaped and childish statuette of an animal and, in the process, find improvement within himself. His intuition (fire) then takes over and prompts him as follows, 'This is exactly what is needed, you must get this introduced into all schools!' Whereupon he is back with his intuitive function (his leading function), seeing all the possibilities there are in modelling, what can be done with it for the welfare of humanity and how, eventually, it can become a way to heavenly experiences. The intuitive type, as usual, drags in the rest of the world, but what he certainly does not do is to dream of sitting down and making himself another statuette. His main function is in the ascendant again and, after a brief but refreshing contact with earth, his feet have left the ground.

Yet it is of the utmost importance for each of us to become aware of the contents of our own inferior functions, even though in practice it would seem that these contents do not become any more manageable in consequence. This fourth function, which is blended with the unconscious, brings with it the whole contents of the unconscious mind as soon as efforts are made to admit it to consciousness. It breaks into the field of consciousness as it were with this undifferentiated material and so leads to either an interaction between consciousness and the unconscious or even, eventually, to their synthesis. Sometimes, owing to the powerful drives associated with this unconscious material, exercising the inferior function can be as devastating in its own way as the proverbial 'bull in a china shop'.

Looked at astrologically, the inferior function is not determined by the position of an element in the horoscope. The main function is decided in this way, of course, but then decides itself where its opposing inferior function will be. However, the vigour with which the inferior function rises into consciousness can in fact have something to do with the position of the elements; also the person in whose horoscope all four elements are equally strong will experience a prolonged inner struggle as the four functions contend for supremacy in consciousness, and the unsuccessful ones will always be more or less accessible to the conscious mind. The fact that the four functions (alias the four elements) are mutually exclusive means that we cannot have more than one outlook on the world at a given moment; that is not to say, however, that we cannot change our outlook from one moment to the next. Thus, supposing a person's superior function is thinking (air) and is under full conscious control, there may be good control too over the ancillary functions (fire and earth) and, if the nature of the inferior function (water) and the conditions in which it manifests are known also, then he may first of all approach an object with his understanding (air), examine it later with his intuition (fire) for hidden possibilities, scan it with his perceptions (earth) and finally evaluate it with his feelings (water) to see whether it is agreeable or disagreeable.

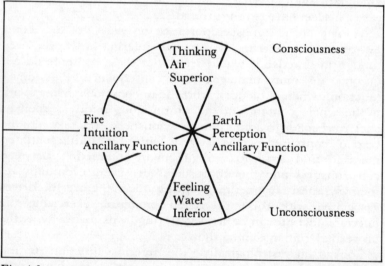

Fig. 4.3

In the above example, the element air or the thinking function is given pride of place and this entails that the inferior function will be represented by the water element. The two intermediate elements (in this case earth and fire) develop into so-called ancillary functions, because they half-surface into consciousness.

Jung's Eight Types

In his book, *Psychological Types*, Prof. Jung divides the human psyche up in two different ways, namely a two-fold way in which the individual responds to external circumstances and a four-fold way in which consciousness assimilates and gives shape to experiences and events. The first division is represented by the concepts of introversion and extroversion and the second by the functions of thinking, feeling, perception and intuition already discussed.

Carl Jung discovered quite early on that observation of the behaviour of different individuals forces us to the conclusion that the activities of some seem determined in great measure by the objects which interest them, while those of others appear to be largely governed by something within themselves, something 'subjective'. Subjectivity is related to objectivity in the same way as the internal is related to everything outside it. So, in this instance, objectivity means those persons, things and events which are located outside the individual (outside the subject) – even though they are no less part of his subjectively perceived universe. The difference between the factors determining a person's activities as set out above stems from the difference known as introversion/extroversion, a difference that, in the last analysis seems to be one of adaptation.

For the introvert, his subjective self (his internal being) is the centre of everything, and the importance of the objective world (everything going on outside him) is judged only to the extent that he is affected by it. The objective stimuli set a mental process in motion which is centred on the innner self. This process, the consequence of a continuing confrontation between his inner, subjective world and objective reality, can be seen as a means of achieving a certain degree of balance between the inner and the outer. The introvert always tries to understand what he perceives and what happens to him and, with this subjective effort, he tries to fit the outer world into his private inner world so to speak.

To a certain extent, the process is reversed in the extrovert individual. For the extrovert, the object, i.e. everything outside himself, is the hub of events. He attaches no value to his subjective inner world. Time and circumstances are his criteria and his inner world is attuned to them. He does what is asked of him by the outside world and lives in accordance with the requirements and standards of the current objective reality. He needs to keep in contact with the outside world and also needs it as a means of self-expression. The extrovert tries to make his subjective world conform to external, objective or factual circumstances. However, the demands of his inner nature (his subjective self) do impose certain restrictions upon him. Conflicts arising between the inner and the outer worlds are reflected in the manner of his adjustment. In so far as external circumstances are a response to his inner condition, the extrovert will be confronted by the demands of his own inner nature. Since his subjectivity is heavily repressed, it wears the features of the unconscious whenever it emerges in his behaviour. The person with an habitually friendly attitude can, at times, offend certain people with sudden fits of unpredictable behaviour. The reactions of these people, who serve as objective entities, provide him with what may be called a reflection of himself by the world outside.

Because of his strong involvement with external matters, the extrovert is dependent on the outside world for recognition and for the unfolding of his possibilities; whereas the introvert, owing to his self-involvement, has more control over the development of his individual potential. In *Psychological Types* Jung writes:

> The one looks at everything from the point of view of personal opinion, the other from that of objective events. These contrasting forms of behaviour are, in the first place, nothing else than mechanisms set to work in opposing directions. We each possess both mechanisms which may be considered as a means of expressing our natural life-rhythm. They have, with good reason, been compared by Goethe to the action of the heart. A rhythmic alternation between the two forms of activity should surely accompany the normal course of existence!

It appears from this that Carl Jung has taken into account that people are not condemned to preserving the same attitude to the external world their life long. On the contrary, he would admit that introversion and extroversion can take one another's places. Nevertheless, he is careful to add that the complex external conditions in which we live, and the probably even more complicated factors determining our individual psychic states, do not permit a completely undisturbed development of our psychic activities except on the rarest occasions. So, too, external circumstances and our inner state very often encourage the operation of the one mechanism while hindering that of the other. Therefore one of the two mechanisms becomes the main one and, if this state of affairs is permanent, we have a 'type', that is to say a regular pattern of behaviour, in which one of the mechanisms reigns supreme, even to the extent that the other one is never able to come to full expression.

No one is either totally extrovert or totally introvert. If they were, then none of us would be able to cope with the constantly changing demands of life and an unbearable mental strain would therefore be imposed on us. A well-defined type never means more than the marked predominance of one of the mechanisms. An individual will usually remain fairly true to type, which does not alter the fact that his conscious attitude cannot undergo a considerable change within a short space of time, as various researches have shown.

Hence conscious attitude is quite different from the functions of consciousness. Whereas the function type gives the specific manner of assimilating and accommodating experience, extroversion and introversion characterize the general psychological behaviour, that is to say, the direction in which the general psychic energy is pointed.

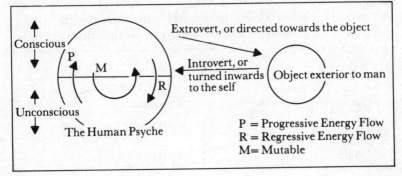

Fig. 4.4

Various directions of psychic energy have already been given in Chapter 3 in connection with the astrological quadruplicities. But there we were concerned with a form of energy flow within the psyche. The psychic energy of which we are speaking in the case of the psychological types has to do with the interchange between the psyche (the subject) and the outer world (the object) and these types mainly stand for the behaviour of the conscious part of the psyche. In short, the psychic energy symbolized by the quadruplicities governs the connection between the conscious and the unconscious parts of the psyche of man; while the psychic energy which has to do with conscious attitudes governs the relationship between the Ego and the outer world.

The two psychological types known as introversion and extroversion, are completely equivalent and compensate one another. They supplement each other. Although a man may be inclined to live his conscious life as an extrovert or an introvert, his unconscious mind has the tendency to turn the opposite way. Thus with an extrovert consciousness, which is mainly orientated to the outer world, we have an introvert unconsicous part of the psyche where everything revolves round the self. Now and again, this unconscious subjective attitude can break through, together with all its archaic, primitive characteristics and then, for example, the positive individual who is the world's friend can suddenly reveal himself as egocentric, critical and grousing, suspicious of everybody and attributing the bases motives to them.

The whole system of conscious attitude and unconscious feed-back is closely connected with the four functions. Thus, the main function, which is situated in the conscious part of the psyche, will follow the consciousness in being either extrovert or introvert. The opposing inferior function will have

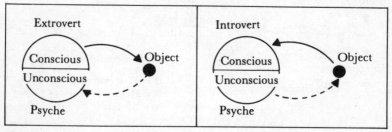

Fig. 4.5

the reverse characteristics. Say a person's attitude is an introvert one and that his superior function is that of thinking, then his inferior function will be feeling and it will have extrovert characteristics. This is in complete agreement with the earlier statement that both mechanisms are present in the human psyche and that, when it is formed, the type is determined only by a *relative* predominance of a given attitude.

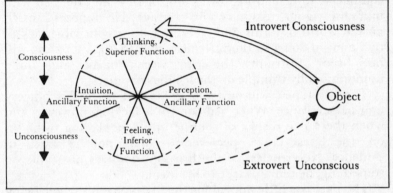

Fig. 4.6

There are then two conscious attitudes which, when combined with the four functions, give us Jung's eight types; each function appears to be able to manifest externally in two ways. So we have in fact the four fundamental categories of the four functions which determine the method of assimilation in the psyche and, as we shall see, are closely connected with the nature of the astrological elements. Just how these functions show themselves in the external world, as introvert or extrovert, is a factor depending on disposition *and* circumstances, making it a much more variable factor apparently than the elements determining the disposition in an astrological sense. Therefore the agreement between element and function stands central to this astrological type theory. The following paragraphs will present a detailed discussion of this agreement, taking each element in turn.

Fire and Intuition

The fire type, comprising the signs of Aries, Leo and Sagittarius, is a type which approaches the world full of enthusiasm and confidence. His impulsiveness and creative expression, coupled with an almost inexhaustible energy and bubbling activity, give this type a productive, acute, inspiring and enthusiastic character. This can, however, degenerate into intrusiveness, aggression, rashness and extravagance.

The fire type is spontaneous and full of self-assurance. He is self-motivated because he is so strongly orientated towards himself. Hence the fire type can make a bad listener. He feels compelled to defend his own point of view and does so with immense vigour, assiduity and courage. He imposes himself on the world of forms and feelings with a noticeable lack of tact and, in doing so (and because he is so impatient and will not brook restraint), he can wreak havoc and quite unintentionally trample on the feelings of others.

The fire type's will-power is great and so are his bravery and perseverance. When self-control is lacking, however, and when there is a dislike of routine and a hankering to be 'in on' the latest craze, perseverance may not be much in evidence. Nevertheless, if the fire sign does set his sights on something, he remains true to his ideal.

The past has little appeal for the fire type – his whole being is in tune with the future and he goes to meet it full of anticipation. New opportunities are always seized with scant recognition of danger; frequently the risks are completely overlooked or are seen only in retrospect. There is a childlike faith that things will turn out for the best which often goes with an underrating of material things – a failure to accord them their true value. When things go wrong, the fire type may display a childish helplessness and outspokenness owing to the extremely powerful impulse to dramatize and exaggerate. It is essential for a person of this type to live in a colourful world of ideals and fantasies. He is only too happy to pursue totally impracticable ideals and visions. In a positive sense this can produce a brilliant mind with much originality, inwardly confident of its own destiny. On the other hand, this means that the fire type is inclined to occupy his time with a quick succession of fantasies and to run the risk of total exhaustion. In addition to aggressive behaviour, pride and arrogance are the negative aspects attending the fire signs.

However, in essence, fire is honest, warm, energetic, strong, care-free, self-assertive, inspired, vital, spontaneous and loyal; if we may so express it, it burns its problems up!

There is a striking similarity between the fire type of classical astrology and the intuitive type distinguished in psychology. The following quotation epitomizes the intuitive type:

'... intuition is neither sensory perception nor intellectual conclusion, and it is not feeling. However, it can make its appearance in these forms.' The perceptions are transmitted by unconscious means and there is, so to speak, an instinctive understanding of what is going on. This intuitive knowledge has the character of certainty and incontrovertibility and it expresses, in imagery and concepts, relationships which are not open to discovery by the other functions of perception, thinking and feeling; or, if they are, only in the most roundabout way. The intuition is mainly unconscious and therefore difficult to explain in words. When the intuitive function takes over to excess, the intuitive type becomes all the more incomprehensible and irrational to those around him; his conscious behaviour is then too much concentrated on and determined by the collective unconscious – which hardly serves the interests of consciousness.

The intuitive type is marked by a certain attitude of expectancy and an unprejudiced and naive outlook on life. The discovery of possibilities can even become a fatal obsession. Trying to turn to account all possibilities which present themselves is mainly motivated by the fact that inspecting possibilities affords the greatest satisfaction to his spirit of anticipation. Things are weighed up and fresh possibilities are sought everywhere and in every situation. Old situations soon become experienced as oppressive and restrictive and the new represents a way of escape from the old. Each object which can afford a means of satisfaction is seized on but, as soon as it has served its purpose, it is thrown overboard as so much ballast. You will not find the intuitive type where things are cut-and-dried but where there are fresh opportunities to be seized, usually with much enthusiasm.

The people around him play a subordinate rôle in the conscious life of the intuitive type and he lends little support to the morale of the community. He is therefore seen as something of a loner with little sensitivity. In fact, he is a sterling fellow with moral values but is led neither by his head nor by his heart. His morality is grounded in reliance on his own inspirations and a willing submission to their power.

Everything can be sacrificed to the opportunity of the moment and the intuitive person prefers to dwell on the world that lies behind material form. That preference sometimes leads to prophetic and profound insights into events in general.

However, this individual rarely sees the connection between his insights and himself, due usually to a want of rational thought. As Carl Jung has commented:

> The remarkable indifference of the extrovert intuitive type to external objects is matched by that of the introvert to internal ones. Just as the extrovert intuitive type constantly scents out new possibilities and hunts them down with no concern for his own comfort or that of others, disregards humane considerations and tears down what has just been built up in his eternal search for change, so the introvert flits from one image to another searching for all the potentialities in the womb of the unconscious without making the connection between the mental phenomena and himself .

It is plain that perception and giving form to his perceptions represents the greatest problem to the intuitive type. When the intuitive function assumes a predominant rôle, the individual concerned is seen to be totally divorced from tangible and material reality, expecially when he is an introvert. What is repressed is the function of awareness of material things, to the extent that, in the extrovert, there is a compulsive urge to attach oneself to certain objects or persons in a way that is completely at variance with the conscious desire for freedom. In more introvert people we see, as unconscious reactions, an immense and irresistible hunger for strong sensory impressions and/or an exaggerated and possessive attachment to the most unlikely objects. Hard reality is the only thing that can help the intuitive person, and the irrational man in general, to escape from the state of inertia engendered by his inner ecstacy. This is especially true of the introvert, in whom the 'fire' turns inwards.

Earth and Perception

For earth types, including the signs Taurus, Virgo and Capricorn, the here and now, the material world and palpable reality take pride of place. It is the world of forms discerned by the physical sense organs and grasped by the practical intellect in which someone of this type feels most at home and on which he reposes his trust. Earth is practical, solid, reliable; therefore its subjects are noted for such qualities as perseverance (not to say obstinacy), industry, patience, caution and control. Just as earth is passive and receptive, so someone of the earth type can do nothing without being motivated and inspired by others, who both incite him to action and help him to assimilate his impressions. For him existence is meaningful largely to the extent that others bring his world picture to life for him. He also has a strong inclination to conform to matter and to become rooted in material possessions. Often a person of this type identifies himself with his possessions or with the part the world expects him to play or with the task it gives him to fulfil.

His reserve (which makes it hard for him to get started) and his tenacity are responsible for the fact that he prefers to maintain conventional behaviour patterns. Because of his formal behaviour and the tendency to identify himself with what is expected of him by the outside world, the earth type can function in the material world with outstanding success. But there is usually a noticeable inability to see and comprehend the abstract and more theoretical side of things.

The presence of a solid standing ground and the acquisition of anything which might offer a firm grasp of affairs is almost a *sine qua non* for his sense of security.

A vision of the connection between things, events and facts is foreign to his nature and so their deeper meaning is often lost on him. To this type belongs the practical scientist who concentrates with efficiency and skill on the phenomena of the material universe. His greatest potential weakness is a limited imagination and a prejudiced point of view. On the other hand, he is capable of hard work and of settling down to a routine.

Because of his poor initiative, coupled with his mistrust and uncertainty of everything that lies outside sensory perception, an individual of this type is generally modest, obliging and tolerant provided there is a basis for trust. Due to his inertia, his longing for certainty and his reserve, he will not willingly waste energy spontaneously or rashly. When he has a goal, he is well placed to exploit his energy effectively and he sticks to that goal with dogged determination. So then, he has a remarkable ability for concentrating and conserving his forces. His conscious efficiency and ability to persevere can impose severe restrictions on self-expression but, when these are not allowed to cramp his style, he has a great capacity for creative work on the material plane. Because his sense of form is so marked, design and construction in physical materials is one of his strong points.

His body plays a big rôle in his life, expecially his health and well-being, since the body is always the direct material envelope of the 'life' that goes on within that body. He has great powers of recuperation. Also, physical experiences and sensuality are important to someone of the earth type.

When we come to compare the 'earth-type' of astrology with the 'perceptive type' of Jungian psychology, we see that they share a pronounced sensorial attachment to objects. There is little or no unconscious cognition or intuition and the most important yardstick for the perceptive type is the intensity of the perceptions occasioned by the object. 'There is no other human type,' says Carl Jung, 'that equals the extrovert perceptive type as far as realism is concerned. His objective sense for fact is unusually well developed. The things he experiences sometimes hardly merit the name "experience".'

The marked instinct for actualities can, it is true, be looked on as very practical, but the perceptive person need not be practical – even irrational 'happenings' based on subjective perception play a part in the perceiving process.

His is a way of life where satisfaction is found in concrete pleasures and everything which is tangible and real is prized. Endeavour and morale are based on this 'enjoyment' of life. However, there is no need for crude sensuality to be involved since the perceptions can become very fastidious. Generally speaking, there is a constant desire to perceive things and physical sensation is not avoided. Whatever is encountered may well be enjoyed without any attempt being made either to reflect on it or to control it. The stimulus must always come from outside, for what comes from within is often neither recognized or understood because of its unreality and incomprehensibility. Carl Jung comments: 'Tangible reality always arouses a person of this type. ... Reality is his ideal and he is very responsive to it. He has no abstract ideas to speak of and therefore no cause to treat any given reality as alien.' He further remarks that the perceptive man is prepared to make sacrifices in order to keep up appearances. Such externals as clothing, good eathing and drinking, fine flavours etc. are important to him.

Although perceptive behaviour involves accepting, without comment or squeamishness, everything that comes along (we are speaking of a non-rational type here), we often find, where the development is negative in character, that what was receptivity has degenerated into hair-splitting and that the moral attitude is rigid and barren. A willingness to accept any religious belief, regardless of creed, can lead to superstitious and magical practices.

We also see, when the perceptive individual is introvert, that although external objects are the most important factors (even in his world) these objects serve merely as stimuli to set further, inner processes in motion – sometimes to the extent that he becomes divorced from physical reality. The introverted perceptive person can find it hard to express himself and often displays a striking sobriety, repose, self-control and passivity; giving the impression that the world of external forms and events has no appeal for him. This impression is created because the reactions evoked by external stimuli become less predictable as the behaviour turns inwards. A patently subjective process at once imparts a strong colouring to all factual perceptions; though such perceptions do remain a necessity for people of this type. This subjective process can sometimes impart a touch of unreality to the activities of one of the introvert perceptive type. Benevolent neutrality is observed and he cultivates a reassuring and conciliatory tone. He is always trying to restore the *status quo*, to calm things down and to preserve the peace. There is no over-enthusiasm, no untoward discouragement; whatever comes along, however unfamiliar it may be, is, in the words of Jung, 'Poured into the proper mould' as far as possible. The effect on others can be rather oppressive. Actually, the individual is much concerned over the influence of the outside world, which he needs to restrain and even to belittle because, in many instances, he is under the unconscious impression that its influence poses a threat to him. Someone of this sort can suffer an imposition but react

with increased resistance and extreme obstinacy next time –
all too often in a far from pacific manner.

People of the perceptive type can consciously express
themselves in artistic and creative work done with the hands,
so as to give the sense organs as much free play as possible.
For the perceptive type, the sense organs are always their most
important means of making contact between the internal and
external worlds. Perception is immediately given and is
therefore not subject to the laws of reason as are the conscious
functions of thinking and feeling.

Air and Thinking

Next in line in our excursion through the signs starting with
Aries, we have, after the earth sign Taurus, the air sign
Gemini.* Air is a connecting element with a rational approach
to facts and events. The air type chiefly emphasizes thinking
in abstract forms, theories, ideas and concepts with a striking
objectivity and liveliness of mind. The gift of expressing
himself in appropriate language, which is so important to a
person of this type, is his in ample measure. It is important
because, with thinking, communication and the exchange of
ideas with others are an indispensible part of his life.

His behaviour is mainly harmonious, friendly and agreeable
and he will accept a mediatory rôle, but can be spoilt by a lack
of firmness and consistency because he seeks peace at any
price due to his strong desire for sociability and harmony.
There is also a certain amount of uncertainty in his thought
and action due to a measure of impersonality and because the
air type can so quickly copy and fit in with the thoughts of
others. This gives the impression that he turns whichever way
the wind blows. There is a tendency to live too much in the
world if ideas and even of dreams, so that in spite of his great
intellectual capacity and well-developed understanding, he
quite often loses sight of reality and of what is practicable.

The air type frequently gives the impression of being cold
and lacking in emotion. The reason is that he needs to test
everything by the laws of logic and to find logical
relationships. Such a person likes to construct a frame of

---

*The original mentions Aries; the other signs have been named in the
translation to make the meaning clear.   *Translator's note.*

reference into which he can fit all experiences, even those involving the feelings not subject to rational processes. By objectifying them and giving them a relative value he can largely free his mind of daily worries.

When the intellectual predisposition is over-emphasized, proportionally less energy is bestowed on deeper emotions. In addition, physical limitations are hardly realized and life is lived in the individual's own abstract and ideal world.

Even in the air type, inspiration comes from outside. Its difference from the earth type lies in the fact that where the earth type is inspired by others, the air type gains inspiration from the *contact* and *exchange* with others. There is great receptivity and there is a real need for inspiration and information in order to keep the process of thinking and communication going. The human type which comes under the heading 'air' is flexible in thought, speech and gesture, is active, industrious, animated, studious, communicative and, above all, uniting. This element is well named the element of 'union', even though the behaviour is undeniably dualistic at times.

It was with the thinking type that Carl Jung found he needed most space in which to explain how it constructs its world picture and self-image. As with all the types, here also he makes the distinction between introvert and extrovert, giving the following description of the extrovert thinking type:

> This is someone who (if he is a fairly pure representative of his type) strives to arrive at understandable conclusions about all his experiences in life; conclusions which, in the end, are again orientated towards objective phenomena in the form either of concrete facts or of general ideas.

Carl Jung said of the introvert thinking type that this type too follows its own ideas but in the reverse direction: from the outer to the inner world. He is more interested in depth than in breadth. The thinking process is central and thinking can be fed as much from subjective and/or unconscious sources as from factual data via the sense organs. Now, thinking always has some standard by which to judge matters. In the extrovert thinking type, this standard is taken from the external world, while in introvert thinkers the standard comes from within and is therefore purely subjective..

In the thinking type we see that all more or less important transactions spring from intellectual and well-considered motives. All actions are subordinated to intellectual conclusions, in which the extrovert thinker finds his bearings in his immediate surroundings and in the world at large. The standards he takes from them are employed to test what is good and what is bad etc. This often rigid formulation (which can frequently be even more rigorous in introvert thinkers), can promote a strict code of morals from which no deviation is permitted. Everything that comes into conflict with it is imperfect and false. When someone of this type tries to force the whole of life into his chosen intellectual formula, he turns into a self-opinionated dogmatist and self-righteous critic, who wants to trammel himself and others in a system. This can have serious consequences for the emotional side of this type. Emotional matters can never be captured in thought constructs; not only because as far as thought is concerned they are the inferior function, but also because they are in general subjective and not amenable to logical treatment and therefore not to be fitted into the formulations of the thinking type. Hence, there is a danger that the thinking type, both extrovert and introvert, will either repress or rationalize his emotional side, leaving his passions, religious sentiments and experiences etc. to live a life of their own in the unconscious mind.

Many times we see that the conscious attitude to life of the thinking type is more or less impersonal; as might be expected from his conscious habit of categorizing everything. We also see that, in consequence, his personal interests suffer in proportion. His health, his social life, his family etc. are accorded scant attention so that he can devote himself to his ideals. When this devotion is carried too far, we may observe a strong inclination to resentment, so that criticisms of the pet system are viewed with suspicion and treated as evidence of spite. However, no single system can embrace the sum-total of reality. Theories become outdated or are revised and even reality itself goes on changing. But often the air type arms himself against the doubt that assails him from outside or springs up within him by adopting a form of fanaticism, and yet this is no more than an over-compensation for the doubt.

In itself, thinking is a creative process which, starting from real objects, leads to fresh facts or to a general summary and synthesis of facts together with a judgement as to their meaning. Carl Jung named as one of the principal characteristics of extrovert thought that it is never devaluing or destructive, but that it always puts a new value in the place of one which has been discarded. This creative aspect is also present in the introvert type, but is less openly expressed; here we see thinking that easily loses itself in the making of theories for their own sake. People of this type find less interest in a conceptual reconstruction of concrete facts. The introvert thinker prefers to turn a vague surmise into a marvellous idea; he collects facts merely as evidence for his own hypotheses and not for the sake of the facts themselves. Propounding questions and theories is at least as important as opening out new perspectives and pressing onwards towards the heart of things.

Just as the extrovert thinker can get bogged down in the multitude of facts with which he surrounds himself, so that he misses their overall meaning, so the introvert thinker runs the risk of being suffocated by a variety of theories and may deny the facts or try to refashion them in accordance with his own fantasies. He can sometimes over-complicate the issue when thinking things out.

Generally speaking then, the thoughts of the thinking type are dependent on objects. Phenomena are brought into (conceptual) relationships and these relationships determine (via a decision-making process) how life is to be lived regardless of suitability. Living in a thought-world of concepts and/ or theories is one of the main reasons why those who belong more to the thinking type display a certain carelessness on the practical and emotional levels.

Water and Feeling

Feelings and deep emotions are characteristic of the signs Cancer, Scorpio and Pisces, which belong to our last element, water. The great emotionality and vulnerability of the water type go hand in hand with its emotional uncertainty and instability. People of this type are easily influenced by their surroundings. However, this should not be regarded as a weakness but as the result of their emotional receptivity and readiness to enter into folk's feelings. One can often guess with

whom they were last speaking or what book they have just
been reading. The ability to put themselves in someone else's
place is so great that, often without knowing it, they quickly
adopt the behaviour and ideas of others.

In spite of this, individuals of the water type frequently have
tremendous forcefulness, which tends to find expression more
on the spiritual than on the physical plane. It would appear
that, in the long term, they do not let others have all their own
way but weild a telling influence of their own.

Quite often, psychic or 'occult' powers are active in the
water type, mostly unconsciously, in the same way that many
of the drives and motivations of this type are buried in the
unconscious mind. The upshot can be the emergence into
consciousness of irrational fears, hyper-sensitivity and strong
reactions to people and places. Even when the water type
seems calm on the surface, a storm can be raging within;
possibly due to the unconscious nature of a personal
motivation already mentioned. A further reason lies in the fact
that the symbolic, like the real water, * has no fixed form and
accepts any given shape quite readily. Thus, the forms
accepted do not always correspond to the essential self of the
water type itself. Becoming aware of the personal desires and
drives and giving form to them is often a slow and painful
process; which is why suffering and patience are frequently
associated with the element water.

There is a great love of solitude, quietness and peace, in
spite of the fact that relationships and human values play such
an important part. The capacity for bringing people together
and for understanding their needs is considerable, together
with deep sympathy and compassion for all who suffer. There
is much unconscious wisdom and insight, making it possible
for individuals of this type to exchange their overpowering
feelings and emotions for an all-embracing love of creation.

Love for one's fellow men and especially for those making
up one's own small circle can be great but, in less developed
water types, this love can become rather possessive and
sentimental and can prove stifling to the recipient in spite of
all the sympathy and good will. The need both to protect and

*The words 'the symbolic, like the real water' replace the words 'water
itself' of the original, to clarify the meaning.   *Translator's note.*

to be protected is clearly present. If unsatisfied, the frustration can show itself in timidity and suspicion until such time as the water type becomes aware of this instinctive reaction.

At the deepest level the water type is questioning, longing, anticipatory and sometimes covetous. Absorption, assimilation, solution and resolution are one and all applicable to the water type, who often fails to discern the aspect of things while wallowing in a welter of feelings. Nor does it try to get down to essentials. Because his motivation is purely emotional, a person of the water type can seldom render a reason for his conclusions; he has much difficulty with thought and logic. Due to the total subjectivity of feelings, an objective approach to life is impossible for someone of the pure water type. What is just as important for him is to become perfectly aware of his own actions. As long as this is not the case, someone of the water type is liable to be taken advantage of by those around him, owing to his deep emotions and his appreciation of the feelings of others as well as to his open altruism.

Although Carl Jung is at pains to point out that there is no way of adequately expressing the feeling process in words, since it cannot be rationalized and does not lend itself to description, he does what he can to say something about it. In the first place, he postulates that feelings are completely subjective interactions between the Ego and other entities such that a certain value is accorded to each entity by way of acceptance or rejection (Jung adds 'and of liking or dislike'). The supplementary 'liking or dislike' forms the basis for value judgements – the rational element in this function.

Mixed with the feelings are emotions arising from the contents of the unconscious and out of former experiences. Extroverted feelings relate to the outside world, from which come their standards of good and evil, beauty and ugliness.

To a certain extent, they lie under the spell of traditional or current values. The attitude of the feeling type can seem insincere to the outside but this is a misapprehension. A person of the extrovert feeling type 'has the feeling that', when he finds something ordinary that is commonly considered beautiful, he is swimming against the tide of the general feeling situation. This, however, is impossible for the extrovert feeling type. Jung says that when, in such circumstances, an extrovert person of this type calls an ordinary-looking thing beautiful, it is an 'effort to fit in' rather than an attempt to deceive. Without this, according to Jung, no pleasant and harmonious life would be possible, this type of person oils the wheels of social, philanthropic and cultural behaviour.

When the attitude described is carried too far, there can be a sort of play-acting pose. Events are approached in an unreliable way with a 'butterfly mind' and the real feelings can no longer be felt. Usually, in such a case, there are unconscious egocentric purposes.

In the extrovert feeling type the feelings are one and all attuned to the external world and its values. For example, a wife is fond of her husband because being so fits in with the pattern of her social existence and she does not examine the matter any further. The feeling is there all right but it carries with it the danger that the personality is completely absorbed by the emotion of the moment: any discordant thought is always turned back into the unconscious as it is about to cross over into the conscious mind. All the same, this does not necessarily mean that people of this type cannot think. Not by any means; it is simply that thoughts which would rob the emotional attitude of its values are rejected.

Since constantly changing and often contradictory emotional situations arise in life, it is not conceivable that this type is always in total sympathy with these situations or able to identify with them. And here is a source of many conflicts: there are many situations in which the personality immerses itself yet unfortunately not all are in agreement with the underlying Ego. At one time the individual is something which he is far from being at others – in appearance anyway, for in point of fact such a shifting personality is something of an impossibility. The basic Ego always stays the same and therefore tends in an opposite direction to the changing states of feeling. To the outsider these can look like a succession of moods and caprices, whereas actually they are all variations on the single theme of the feeling-type Ego. These moods can evoke so much resistance in the unconscious of this person that there is an increasing likelihood that he will overcompensate by saying things he does not really mean. A slight change in a given situation can then upset the balance of the Ego in the opposite direction so that a diametrically opposed viewpoint is adopted. All this happens in complete sincerity and so the extrovert feeling type is extremely likely to suffer not only alienation from his immediate circle, even while he experiences an overwhelming need to maintain close emotional ties with those around him.

The more introvert feeling type is also misunderstood quite often. Not in this case because of a too obvious and seemingly senseless compliance with others but because of a high degree of uncommunicativeness bordering on apparent indifference. The depth of the feelings can only be surmised, for the fairly unapproachable bearing makes them inaccessible to the observer. The mask that is worn is often childish and/or commonplace while the impression is given that within all is more or less harmonious and peaceful. However, nothing could be further from the truth. It is because the introvert feeling type has the greatest difficulty with the external expression of feelings that he is often considered to be cold, remote and unfeeling.

When the feeling type has slight control over internal events, overcompensation can occur in the shape of a consuming ambition and of vanity, tyranny and bullying, so that those around experience a stifling atmosphere. The thinking can then develop primitive traits, expressing themselves as concretism and a slavery to facts, and there is a possibility that the individual will imagine that he feels what other folk are thinking, not realizing that this is completley subjective. So we see that suspicion, distrust, intrigue etc. is not foreign to the feeling type. Nevertheless the intensity and depth of what is experienced and felt, on whatever level, cannot be put into words.

Man and the Elements

There are very many imtermediate forms which, in practice, can confuse the issue when we come to study the four types mentioned above. These may reveal themselves in the horoscope in the way in which the elements are placed. Now the points of agreement between the experimental data of Carl Jung, as expressed in his work on types, and the traditional astrological elements seem to be so strikingly close, that we can use the dynamics of the types and their action in order to gain more insight into the operation of the elements in the horoscope.

There is certainly no need to suppose that the strength of a certain element in an individual will emphasize the characteristics of the types described above. It is perfectly possible that, owing to circumstances, a certain function or element (as the case may be) which is clearly stressed in the horoscope will be underemphasized or, if it is in fact the most important function, another less important element will supplant it temporarily or permanently. In that event, the most important element will not exhibit the creative characteristics shown in the more or less pure type, but will be less controlled and more unconscious in its expression. Also a function type can be so pronounced that the picture is not clear-cut due to unconscious overcompensation. In other cases, the elements are so spread that any kind of typing is difficult, or else we see that two contrary elements, e.g. thinking-air and feeling-water are both pronounced. This means that a struggle for supremacy in the psyche of the person concerned develops between the two elements and , as said earlier, this, when understood, can lead to great insight into the tensions that this person creates in and around himself.

A number of factors are involved in determining the type in question and, among other things, it is wrong to do no more than count the number of planets occupying each element in order to work out the 'strength' of the latter. The places of the sun, moon and ascendant are very significant and the positions of their dispositors are also important. In our culture, where thought is held in high esteem, Mercury often plays a decisive rôle; and so the culture in which a person lives must always be taken into account, even if as no more than a background influence.

Although a number of circumstances and facts can be inferred from a horoscope as it stands, type determination is very difficult. It is true, of course, that developmental tendencies can be given from which the individual is free to choose; to decide, in other words, which function shall be his superior one. But very many factors play a part in this development and it is certainly not true that the individual has to develop as his superior function the one to which he is most strongly inclined. Psychologists have proved in detail how people can throw dust in their own eyes and how hard it is to gain an insight into the workings of one's own psyche. The psychological function with which one operates has a lot to do with these workings.

For an astrologer, it is the elements which give him a key to discovering the potentials and capabilities of the enquirer as well as the possible conflicts within his psyche. This enables him to offer advice on how the individual can shape his life in conformity with his psychic structure. Naturally, it is much more difficult to decide what a person ought to do when the way in which the elements are disposed gives rise to much conflict. It is possible that, owing to certain experiences, someone cannot realize his best potential but has to develop a weaker element. Here is a simple example. Say somebody has the sun in Sagittarius and the moon in Leo, with Mercury in conjunction with Saturn in Capricorn. The fire-earth or intuition-perception conflict is very strong. This person is essentially inuitive but, owing to the placement of Mercury, he has an entirely different way of approaching facts and phenomena; that is to say a very concrete one which is in oppositon to the background influence of his sun and moon. If he chose the career of taxation official, he could perhaps do well; yet there would be insufficient support from his sun and moon placements and this could occasion an unconscious compensation or give rise to feelings of dissatisfaction. On the other hand, should he choose to go in for private enterprise, he not only would need all kinds of opportunities (intuition) but also would require to know that everything was contained within safe and solid limits (the Capricorn influence). The second course of action would give him a better chance of developing in accordance with his natural bent. In the example chosen, the decision largely rests with the individual himself, in spite of adverse circumstances. His decision (whether or not taken consciously) will determine the kind of life he is going to lead within the scope of his possibilities and also, of course, what psychological function will be most strongly emphasized. And so, there is no law that says that what is in the horoscope must be developed; quite often all too many gifts and possibilities are allowed to slumber.

A development which runs counter to the inherent qualities can lead to neuroses. Sigmund Freud defined a neurosis as a disharmony in the organization of the Ego. Jung went further and said that, in fact, a neurosis is a stop signal given when the wrong road is being taken and a shout of warning in the personal recovery process. In this connection we can distinguish two processes capable of producing neuroses.

i) Too great an emphasis is laid on the superior function, preventing the other elements from developing to any extent, if at all, and compelling the inferior function to try and overcompensate more and more strongly. Thus there is interference with the superior function from the uncontrollable regulatory activities of the unconscious. The possible over-strong differentiation and its compulsive character is something that can create big problems later in life and a one-sidedness which will cry out for solution.

ii) A person with an obvious inclination towards a certain function who is unable to develop it for some reason or other but has to find expression in an ancillary or even in the inferior function, can suffer from a true neurosis. The function that is developed and used will always display primitive and archaic traits and, because of its ungovernability at times, it will more than once land the person concerned in serious difficulties. There are plenty of examples of people who, with perfectly sincere motives, do the exact opposite of what ought to be done in a given situation, so that things turn out quite differently from what they had intended. If some element is strongly represented in a horoscope without apparently making much of a showing in the subject's character, this could indicate an incorrectly 'chosen' and developed superior function. Usually, such a choice is unconscious and, in many instances, is more the result of a combination of education, circumstances, the culture in which the person is brought up and his personal inclinations, as already described. However, the personal inclinations tip the scales either for or against the formation of a neurosis over a wrong 'choice' of main function.

The scheme in which the elements are representatives of the

psychological functions is one of the bases of psychological astrology and confirmation of its correctness may be found in various astrological books. Thus, A.E. Thierens writes: 'But people whose power lies in the fire signs often underestimate the value of the earth signs which provide them with the motif, the materials and the opportunity for expressing their initiative, an undervaluation which springs of course from the feeling of self-determination.' It would be hard to find a clearer statement of the contrast between the intuitive and the perceptive functions.

Insight into and understanding of the elements and their psychic functions is indispensable for the correct interpretation of a horoscope and for a true judgement of comparative horoscopes. In addition, it can help us to realize that reality may be approached in different manners and that another's appreciation of reality can have as much justification as our own and that all the forms of experiencing reality are necessary for achieving a balance.

5

The Zodiac as a Path of Life

The Significance of the Concepts 'Zodiac' and 'Dierenriem' or 'Tierkreis'

All nature finds expression in cycles of becoming, being and dissolution, and the human race, as a part of nature, is inescapably involved in these cycles. The metamorphosis observable in the course of a year here on earth appears to be symbolized in the succession of signs in the zodiac which, as we have already seen, no longer corresponds to the actual constellations as they appear in the heavens. The interlocking band of the twelve signs is known in The Netherlands and Germany as the 'dierenriem' or 'Tierkreis' respectively. We call it by the Greek word 'zodiac'.

These words have an air of mysticism about them. Thus it is frequently stated that the meaning of the word 'zodiac' is 'path of life'. The first time the term zodiac was put in writing in any form, so far as we can tell, was by Aristotle (who lived in the fourth century B.C.). He spoke of a circle of animals (or, in a wider sense, 'living creatures') and used the word 'zooidion'. The derivative, 'zooidiakos' is found again later and usually as an adjective qualifying a noun such as 'hodos' (= way) or 'kuklos' (= circle); it seldom appears alone. So 'zodiac' means nothing more than circle of animals.

It is in the German-speaking areas, in particular, that the suggestion has gained currency that the German word for the zodiac, 'Tierkreis' (which, like the cognate Dutch word, 'dierenriem' seems also to mean no more than 'circle of animals') is really a corruption of Tyr-kreis. The essential meaning of the rune, Tyr, is eternal change, from annihilation to rebirth. As we learn from old North-German tradition, Tyr

was a son of the sun god, Wodan (or Odin), and was called
The Reborn, who made his appearance as the rejuvenated sun
god after the self-offering of Wodan. The story goes that
Wodan hanged himself on a branch of the World Tree,
Yggdrasil, and awoke from a nine-day trance, reborn as Tyr;
so that Tyr is the symbol of death and rebirth and hence the
perpetual round of change and cycle of life. According to R.J.
Gorsleben, the rune Tyr (↑) also stands for the numerical
value twelve. There are twelve signs of course.*

Whether we look at it linguistically or historically, this
explanation of 'Tierkreis' as meaning 'Tyr-kreis' (the circle of
Tyr) has scarcely any scientific value. Nevertheless, although
'the zodiac' and 'der Tierkreis' seem to have no deeper
significance as words, this does nothing to detract from the
symbolism behind the names of the signs. The deep
symbolism behind the signs adopted from the astronomical
constellations does justify us in treating the zodiac
symbolically as a 'path of life' and in styling it as such.

This path of life is composed of our twelve modern signs
(anciently there were fewer) which correspond to stages of
development in human life and in nature as a whole. In his
Pulse of Life, Dane Rudhyar claims that the inner emotional
and biological changes in human nature are very closely
linked with the external changes in flora and fauna. This was
already felt by early man in his close contact with nature and
is still relied on by various schools of astrology as evidential
support.

It is generally agreed that astrology took its rise in the
Northern Hemisphere; so it seems highly likely that nature's
phases of growth in this hemisphere have laid the foundations
of the view of life held by the populations living there, who,
building on their experiences, slowly constructed the
astrological frame of reference that is still used today. And so,
the content of the concepts represented are as liable to
development and change as is humanity itself; which is why
the meaning contained in astrology has gained new
dimensions and wears a different aspect from the one it had
earlier. Astrology has the vitality to come to terms with the

*Additional note added by translator to make the meaning clear.

latest trends in our day and age.

Not only do the twelve signs of the zodiac represent twelve different character types; more than this, they are symbols of certain energies in harmony with the 'vibrations' belonging to various times of year. Assuming that the principle of synchronicity is true, these factors can be linked together. As Carl Jung says, '... everything born or done in this moment of time carries within it the quality of the moment.' When the sun occupies a certain sign at birth so that, in popular jargon, the native is said to 'be' that sign, it does not mean that the native will necessarily display the characteristics of that sign; what it does mean is that, in the depths of his being, the individual concerned will experience the impulse to become conscious of his disposition and character while expressing them and developing them in accordance with the nature of the sign. So then, the twelve signs of the zodiac lay down twelve different 'paths of life', each of which has its constructive and its destructive sides. However, it is certainly a mistake to talk of good and bad, difficult and easy signs in this connection. Each sign is essential to the whole chain, each sign logically proceeds from the one before it and forms a logical preparation for the one that follows. Every sign has its own manner of expression, both in a higher and in a lower sense, and it depends on the person himself which options he will take and how he will use them.

All twelve signs of the zodiac can be found in each horoscope chart, from which fact we may infer that, in essence, each one of us has all the properties of the path of life within him. It is the individual horoscope in which certain points are emphasized and this horoscope indicates which factors will play a rôle in the life of the individual and to what extent they will do so. In itself, the fact that all signs (and all planets) are contained in the birth horoscope, tells us that the twelve signs of the zodiac, irrespective of which of them holds the sun, symbolize archetypally the individual and the collective life process.

The twelve paths of life or, from another point of view, the twelve stages of growth, are not peculiar to astrology. If we take a close look at Christian tradition, we see that the twelve apostles are in some respects representative of twelve human types. The apostles have a marked resemblance to the signs of the zodiac. The number twelve is also found in the twelve sons of Jacob, the ancestors of the twelve tribes of Israel. Nor should we forget the twelve gates of the New Jerusalem as described in the Book of Revelation.

An important part is played by the number twelve in other cultures too. Thus Vedic lore has its twelve Adityas, or twelve aspects of the 'God of the Solar Path', who manifest, in this cultural context, as twelve divine beings with diverse properties. G.H. Mees says they are best interpreted as various stages along the spiritual path within the Vedic tradition and that then the parallel with astrology as studied in the West becomes clear. The twelve labours of Hercules, and twelve 'houses of the Aesir' in Germanic mythology, are representations of identical factors in the human collective unconscious. They present themselves to us in different modes as archetypal ideas but, in essence, they are designations of the twelve stages of growth in nature and of the twelve paths of life in man. In astrology they are enshrined in the twelve signs of the zodiac.

The Sequence of the Signs

Contained in the sequence of positive and negative signs is the series of cardinal, fixed and mutable crosses, which manifest in a fourfold way, analogous to the elements fire, earth, air and water. A combination of these quadruplicities and elements results in twelve different units which, as already explained in Chapter 2 are mutually exclusive. Although certain signs, e.g. those belonging to the same element, may display similarities, there is always an essential difference between one and another.

An exhaustive type description detailing all possible characteristics of each sign lies beyond the scope of this book. Adequate material of this type is to be found in other books on astrology. Here we shall concentrate our attention on the sequence of the growth-stages and the directions taken by psychic energy seen in conjunction with the four different methods of orientation (or function types). In this way we shall attempt to forge a link between ancient doctrine and modern psychology.

Aries – the Ram

positive quadruplicity: cardinal
element: fire
day ruler: ♂
night ruler: ♁

In the Aries phase, we seen an awakening and the first step taken by the individual consciousness out of the undifferentiated ocean of the unconscious. The 'primal scream' and heat of the fire element are impulsive and direct. The need to be always starting something new and to be a pioneer are clearly expressed by the fact that this cardinal sign is also a fire sign. The sign of the Ram is the sign of the beginning and of the desire to press forward. In nature, this outgoing impulse is visible in seed germination, which marks the start of spring in the Northern Hemisphere.

As a fire sign, Aries belongs to the intuitive type, predominantly progressive psychic energy – creative and 'ready for anything'. Whether or not the Aries subject always finishes what he starts is another matter. The powerful urge towards outward expression means that the Ram displays many of the characteristics of the psychological function of intuition. There is a childishly impressionable and anticipatory attitude to life; always searching for new possibilities. As soon as a situation has settled down into some form of regularity, it is suddenly seen as restricting because, in this stage, the freedom for unfettered manifestation and personal discovery is given priority. An individual of the Ram type can become the slave of his own craving for independence and liberty and that is something which, during the course of his life, he must learn to bring under control or to conquer. Most of his energies are devoted to the idea of emancipation, just as the seedling breaks out of the seed and strikes a path through the soil to the upper air to find a place of its own. In much the same way, the Aries native slowly learns his limitations in the process of self-manifestation and of living in the sign of individualism. This process usually runs a tempestuous course and he may expect to be told that he will never learn until he has burnt his fingers. Nevertheless, the Aries phase is an essential part of human development. It involves living from inside to outside and, since it symbolizes 'the beginning', it marks the commencement of a voyage of self-discovery. This developmental stage is one devoted to the expression of self and for which reason the Ram type often exhibits egotistic traits, showing little interest in the thoughts and feelings of others. The indifference is not deliberate, rather there is an inner compulsion towards self-determination. For one of the Ram type all things are possible, since he has yet to encounter fixed structures and boundaries. Consequently, he is pre-eminently a fighter for the ideas welling up within him. His audacity, activity and enthusiasm stand him in good stead, although they can degenerate into acerbity, violence and indiscretion.

As an essentially intuitive type, the Ram is far ahead of his time; however, the temptation to meddle and the longing to give expression to endless ideas can lose him the sympathy of others. The compuslion to start many things can also reveal itself in the way someone of the Aries type will alter his opinion from one moment to the next and, with typical enthusiasm, adopt a standpoint diametrically opposed to his former one, defending the new with as much fire and verve as as he had defended the old. He is extremely inquisitive and much given to experiment, so that his interest in a project will often flag while he turns to something fresh.

On account of the fact that the Aries person has yet to learn his limitations, and because he can recklessly play with fire without realizing it, he is capable of rushing headlong into all kinds of trouble. The courage and daring ascribed to Aries are not so much a conscious determination to brave any danger as the effects of a primary life-impulse which sees no danger. It is the possibilities within a dangerous situation that are seen, and this, combined with his lack of appreciation of his own limitations, makes an individual of the Aries type the intrepid pioneer *par excellence* and a leader who will stop at practically nothing. Ambition and the competitive spirit (he wants to be best in everything) arising from the discovery in early youth that he is the sort of individual who has to prove himself, are an added spur. Physically, too, the Ram can have natural advantages; his recuperative powers are very great in all respects.

In the Aries phase, man learns that he is an individual on this earth and, at the same time, by his setbacks and recoveries, he learns where his options and limitations lie. Once he has come to terms with this phase, he can rejoice in a self-trust adequately based on his own inner resources and develop a large measure of integrity. Without being too dogmatic about it, he can keep faith with a deep-felt conviction of his task in life and do what he has to do without fuss and bother.

Taurus – the Bull

negative quadruplicity: fixed
element: earth
ruler: ♀

In the Taurus development phase, a direction is imparted to the scattered impulses of Aries. A methodical and practical shaping occurs in order to create the secure basis which was obviously neither present nor necessary in the Aries phase. We can see how important a part is played by the process of formation when we look at nature itself (especially in the month of May in the Northern Hemisphere). Somewhat similarly, the human psyche in the Taurus phase is strongly inclined towards the formative side of life. Since it is a perceptive type, external forms and materials loom large in the life of this sign. The world of ideas and ideals of the previous sign, Aries, is hardly, if at all, understood. In the Taurus phase, the individuality is established and the boundaries circumscribing the individual possibilities are known and well-defined. The subject knows his limitations. The main theme in the new phase is the search for forms of secure existence for his individuality.

Just as the Ram type identifies with his freedom and urge to do things, so the Bull type reaches self-consciousness in the first place by grasping at mainly material values. This can express itself as a great desire to own everything thought to be of value and not necessarily as fluttering round one's partner and friends and fussing over them. Another possibility for expression is the use of material things for creative work. In this way, although the world of material forms retains its importance, the individual develops from subordinating his own craving for security on the material plane to subordinating matter to himself.

As a perceptive type within the fixed quadruplicity, man in this phase is capable of great tenacity and has an almost proverbial ability to settle down in practical and profitable affairs. The inner-directed psychic energy enables prolonged retention of images, concepts and matter. Someone of the Taurus type can, as a reliable and stabilizing factor, ensure that much is completed which others have given up in despair. On the other hand, the lack of flexibility in thought and in outlook on life, the pronounced tendency to keep to the safe path and to avoid new pathways as much as possible, and the wish to hold on to what he has, can turn him into a 'bit of an old fossil'. All this is obviously a reaction against the previous (Aries) phase, in which imprudence, a sense of adventure and initiative are the keywords. In the Taurus phase, it is prudence, keeping to the known and passivity that are most in evidence. The result is that after the Ram has long since left the stage, the Bull is still there working out the implications of the Aries initiatives, giving them form and is putting the practical value of the Aries ideas to the test.

In the emotional sphere, too, the Bull represents a reaction to the Ram. The Ram type is very quickly stimulated but disappointments are soon forgotten. Fresh possibilities seem to stretch out endlessly in life. In contrast to this, the Bull type's reactions are much slower and he can dwell on his disappointments to the end of his days. To the extent that the Ram can be unconsciously faithless so does the Bull stay consciously true, mainly on account of his need for security.

Since his psyche is orientated in a perceptive manner, the Taurus type concentrates mainly on material pleasures whether sensual or purely artistic. Nevertheless, the impulse must always come from outside and this may give an impression of laziness. All the same, the Taurean native can work hard and long.

The retentiveness inherent in the fixed cross often comes over as a great sense of economy, which is closely connected with the pronounced need for security. That is why the Taurean is in his element in practical callings. He has a close liaison with matter and appreciates its value.

Gemini – the Twins

positive quadruplicity: mutable
element: air
ruler: ☿

After the beginning phase of Aries has been translated into security and form in the phase of Taurus, a further reaction occurs in the phase of Gemini. For example, Taurus is domesticated but Gemini takes little care of his home or is never in it. In this stage, there is no longer any commitment to material objects. There is, however, a compelling need to connect objects with one another or to form links between external objects which can be as varied as men and things and as facts and ideas. In this phase, man steps for the first time outside the world of his individual possibilities and certitudes. This first step outside takes Gemini into what, at first glance, looks like a disordered and disorganized world. On this basis, we may explain the need to first relate things to what is known and then to find mutual relationships between things and then bring them into some sort of order, as no more than a natural reacton to what is new. As thinking is the function with which the Gemini type (an air type) finds its bearings in the world, the logical faculties come to the fore in all circumstances. The personal confidence of someone of this type derives from an intellectual ability to dissect and arrange whatever is encountered, regardless of whether it is concrete or abstract. With his manner of connected thinking, which is restless and very mobile, an individual of the Gemini type can see all sides and so is the inventor of systems and techniques without, however, getting down to the fundamentals of what he meets on his pathway through life.

Taking into consideration that Gemini is a positive sign, we can see that the direction taken by the psychic energy (which can be just as easily progressive as regressive) has an outward-going, progressive tendency, so that the mobility makes its appearance quite noticeably. The same mobility is found once more in the contacts made by someone of the Twins type. He requires many contacts for the formation and development of his character, though not necessarily of the deep friendship variety.

Mobility takes a positive direction and gives to this type a certain degree of vivacity, versatility and changeableness, which can prove very useful to its members professionally if they go in for work involving the communication of either thoughts or things – say in journalism or trade.

The inconstancy observed here, in emotions, ideas and occupations, is a reaction to the Taurus phase. The tendency to be impersonal makes someone of this type step light-heartedly over things of value to which the Bull with all his jealousy and possessiveness would hold tight. At the same time, this is the first stage in which man is conscious of his position *vis-à-vis* the outside world, and that is where the duality of the Twins comes in. The outer world arouses his curiosity and captures his attention, but the multiplicity of things, all of which appear to have equal importance, leads him to skip from one subject to another. His concentration is easily broken and he seldom finds an opportunity to develop his thoughts. Analogous to the multifarious unfolding of nature in the flowering of the year, there are the great many sides of Gemini type. The many-sidedness and changeableness impart to this type enormous adaptability but bring with them the dangers of superficiality and dilettantism. But once again the duality of this type comes to the fore in its adaptability. The individual watches himself facing the universe and his adjustment to the outside switches to an inner adjustment. The neutral stance and the need to bring order and make connections, flow in essence from inner uncertainty as to the individual's place in the world. So much attention is paid to the outside world and so much interest is bestowed upon it that the inner world is left in a state of considerable passivity – values are sought in the immediate environment. So, in this phase of development, man must learn the lesson that he has to be himself and to have the courage of his opinions without hiding behind impersonal mental constructs derived from the world outside. Mental perception of the universe is the keynote of the Gemini phase.

Cancer – the Crab

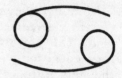

negative quadruplicity: cardinal
element: water
ruler: ☽

In the phase of Cancer the apex of the first part of the growth process of man is reached. After the initial action (Aries) and consolidation (Taurus) and the setting up of a relationship with the outside world (Gemini), we have the influence of the outer on the inner in the form of impressions and feelings. The element Water, which corresponds to the psychological function of feeling, alerts us by its attribution to the sign Cancer that personal growth will proceed by way of inner experience. In spite of the fact that Cancer is one of the cardinal signs, which indicates an outward flowing energy, this cardinal-sign aspect is not so obvious because Cancer already belongs to the negative, inward-looking signs. This intimates the presence of a degree of duality in the emotional life of the Cancer type, so that, while there is great self-involvement with a great deal being experienced internally and in silence, an equally powerful involvement is felt in what is going on outside. The Crab literally is 'much attracted' and is attractive in turn. The fact that the Crab native does not in principle like to make himself conspicuous and prefers to live in his own domestic and emotional privacy, means that he can well be the driving force behind someone else. It is in this way that the cardinal cross impulse to force the pace in the outside world is often manifested. On the one hand, the immediate circle may resent this meddling with their affairs but, on the other hand, the participation of the Cancer individual may prove stimulating.

His wealth of emotions and his inclination to assimilate impressions from the outer world via his feelings means that someone of the Cancer type has a great need of emotion, intimate experiences and of petting and pampering. By way of reaction to Gemini, which is so much involved in the world and so little involved in itself, Cancer takes for its main sphere of activity the home and domestic affairs together with the family and tradition. Family and parenthood are tremendously important to this type, which thus presents a parallel to the fruiting season in nature.

The emotional side of the Cancer character is hard to put into words. It reveals itself in great imagination, sensibility and attachment, and the Cancer subject has no difficulty in expressing his feelings in artistic productions. As a water sign, Cancer is very active internally even though considerable passivity is displayed towards the outside. This can show itself as affection, friendliness, openness to impressions and amenableness; though also as despondency, self-indulgence and self-pity. Owing to his great sensitivity, what is said and done by others is often taken the wrong way.

His feelings are not only the spectacles through which the Cancer individual looks but also the tool he must learn to handle. In human development, the Crab phase means that emotions aroused by the environment have to be assimilated and that the inner, emotional side of life has to be recognized and understood; because man cannot function perfectly without it.

In this, the first of the water signs, an overcompensation for the vulnerability of the feelings is often seen in the shape of an ostentatious display of feelings and emotions. The insecurity entailed in this vulnerability is overcompensated by fits of pique and, in extreme cases, by staging pathetic scenes. The reactions of those around can then act as a pleasing stimulus and the individual can easily be tempted to start 'doing it for kicks'. Possessiveness towards relatives and children is also a result of this insecurity; the fear of losing the external forms that satisfy the need for emotional experiences brings out the caring, cherishing and mothering side of the Cancer type. The changing moods to which the Cancer type is liable may also be attributed to this insecurity.

When, in the Cancer phase, man has come to an understanding acceptance of his own feelings, he is already for the next cycle of the elements, starting with the fire again in the phase of Leo.

Leo – the Lion

positive quadruplicity: fixed
element: fire
ruler: ☉

In the first four phases, we saw how different sides of the individuality were developed. The possibilities and limitations of the individuality were explored and established, then the outer world was investigated and it was allowed to work on the inner nature in the form of emotions and feelings. In the next phase, we have an individual personality which is conscious of itself. In the phase of Leo, the leading theme is the 'dramatic' presentation of the personality as a means of gaining recognition.

In this phase, the individual has become sure of his identity yet is still very unsure of himself in the social arena. Consequently, by making himself out to be someone big, he tries to ensure for himself the place in society to which he is only entitled in his imagination. After the formation of the personality in the first four signs, the renewed series of elements has to do with the social behaviour of the personality and chiefly with its further cultivation. The first step in this direction is taken in the phase of the Lion. The developed self-consciousness, which is much more 'conscious' than is that of the Ram (self-consciousness is a trait of the intuitive types and signs), is strongly turned in on the self. Leo belongs to the fixed cross and so the pyschic energy has a pronounced inward flow. Here is an explanation of the fact that, although Leo is one of the positive signs and is also a fire sign, the Leo type makes an impression of great stability; it does not run out of steam as quickly as the Aries type tends to do and is much better placed to finish what it starts.

The self-involvement of the fixed cross, in combination with the strong self-expression common to fire signs, explains the great need (though not absolute necessity) experienced by Leo to be the centre of attention; above all he feels himself to be a born leader of authority. Thus the Leo type is eminently suitable as a director, chairman or the like; positives which mean a lot to him because they can bring the social recognition that confirms his sense of personal worth.

With his intuitive orientation, Leo is often well ahead of his time, even though he is particularly good at fitting in with current trends; he attaches great importance to a rôle in social life in the widest sense of the world. Since his energy is directed inwards, he is usually saved from the ruptures in relationships commonly the result of the impulsiveness peculiar to the fire signs.

Owing to his social uncertainty, someone of the Leo type can overcompensate by taking the attitude that, come what may, he will be the centre of attention and, in doing so, stir up a great deal of opposition. Sweeping gestures, ostentatious jewellery and luxury living serve to underline the situation. Whenever a power complex develops in this way, the things mentioned can end in tyranny, stubborness, passionate behaviour and haughtiness. On the other hand, Leo's great stability can produce resoluteness and valour and make him chivalrous, magnanimous, sympathetic and idealistic.

In the Leo phase, we observe that after his personality has been formed, man sets to work on himself. Hobbies and other forms of creative self-expression are taken up at this stage. In nature, the fruit is ripe and ready for picking; cropping can begin. Surface ripeness is found in the sign Leo, which is analogous to the heat of summer. However, in human development, inner ripeness comes in winter.

The intensity with which someone of the Leo type is aware of his own personality and the resulting pride and will-power with which he meets life can give him the feeling that he has much to offer – a feeling that can produce great liberality. In return for his gifts, the Leo type expects a certain amount of devotion and appreciation. In this stage of development, man runs the risk of becoming the victim of his ideals and illusions while intoxicated with self-experience; because in this state he fails to see that hankering after and dreaming of social acceptance subtly separates him from his ideal.

The bold approach to what lies outside is a reaction to the stay-at-home Crab; although the Lion can be domestic too, just so long as he can turn his house into a centre where friends and acquaintances can meet and where he can satisfy his hankering for pleasure, games and amusement and give full rein to his creativity.

Virgo – the Virgin

negative quadruplicity: mutable
element: earth
ruler: ☿

The Virgo phase is both a consequence of and a reaction against the high point of the Leo phase, in which self-consciousness, self-expression and concentration on broad issues were the main themes. In the present phase, discrimination is developed, based on the critical analysis of the consequences of actions and transactions such as come to the fore in the Leo phase. Even the fiery emotions and passions of the Leo native are subjected to a critical analysis in the phase of the Virgin, so that this sign makes an impression of coldness. This is actually a reaction against the display of self-assurance in the Leo phase. In the Virgo phase, man feels his own vulnerability and learns to see his own faults; so self-criticism is an important factor at this stage. His own motives and desires are subjected to constant analysis, so that the Virgo type is difficult to handle. As a negative sign, Virgo turns inwards, and yet the psychic energy is fairly free-flowing. As a mutable sign, the Virgin presumably conceals considerable liveliness behind her mask of coldness, but her spritely mind finds it difficult to express itself in the outside world.

In the phase of this, the second earth sign, the phenomenal world is approached with the function of perception (just as it is in the Taurus phase); the individual is preoccupied with tangible reality and prefers to deal with concrete and material things. However, in this phase, attention is not devoted to the acquisition of whatever offers security, as was true of the Taurus phase, but to gaining an insight into the diversity of forms and motives. The mobility of the psychic energy introduces a measure of uncertainty into some sides of the personality, and so the Virgo type is kept busy making a critical evaluation of her personality with a view to devaluing herself so to speak; much as the Gemini type, the first of the mutable signs, is always playing down his own opinions in his eagerness to snatch at the latest idea. This self-depreciation holds the reason for the modesty (or fear of being noticed) and shyness of the Virgin (whereas the stir and bustle of Gemini tend to attract attention).

Virgo's perceptiveness makes her very fond of comfort, good clothes, fine and healthy food etc. What is more, with her practicality and the detailed way in which she looks at the world, she is a good planner; nothing escapes her attention and she has a strongly-developed sense of proportion.

The ability to analyze plus lively thinking fit this type of practical and detailed scientific research; as the kind of researcher who can spend much of life on a very specialized project in quiet seclusion (due to the negative side of the sign!). A methodical approach, desire of knowledge, orderliness, acumen and sobriety are virtues which assist the Virgo type in this work.

The reaping commenced under Leo reaches full harvest in Virgo; a harvest culled from the growing insight into motivations. There is a close connection here with the subservience ascribed to the sign of Virgo. On account of the difficulty experienced in dealing with affairs, the Virgoan works best in a subordinate position; but, in trying to achieve self-understanding the ability has been gained to show understanding to others. When further differentiated, this type is in a position to serve humanity without at the same time thinking of self or personal advantage.

The perfection that Virgo looks for in herself is also sought in others and perhaps this is one reason why so many unmarried people come under this type. Her very cold, aloof and unemotional behaviour enables someone of the Virgo type to analyze and categorize facts in an extremely objective and intellectual manner; the findings are then handed out to others in a rather pedantic fashion.

Virgo's purity and craving for perfection have much to do with the feeling of uncertainty which, in another respect, is the driving force behind the urge to analyze. The hypersensitive 'don't-touch-me' attitude in love affairs, however, is as much a matter of fastidiousness as of insecurity. Yet if insecurity does play too big a part in affairs of the heart, refuge can be taken in overcompensation. In that case either too much is demanded of the partner (who must be ideal) or else the Virgo individual lapses into out-of-character behaviour. Needless to say, chastity is no longer evident in the last instance. Even then, Virgo is not deserted by her critical faculties, however.

The Virgo phase is the phase of self-criticism and self-perfection, although less developed Virgoans certainly do not take kindly to critical remarks. This is the consequence of a keenly felt inner vulnerability. In the Virgo phase, this vulnerability is submitted to a searching examination with a view to preparing for participation, initially with a partner (the phase of Balance), in the greater whole. Introspection and refining are central to the development phase of the Virgin.

Libra – the Balance

positive quadruplicity: cardinal
element: air
ruler: ♀

One of the turning-points in human development, as expressed in the phase of Libra, is associating with others, and in particular a partner, on an equal footing. The phase of critical analysis (and of self-criticism) has run its course in Virgo and will now be put to good use. Contrasts in general come into prominence and the Libra type spares no pains in striking a balance between any items which appear to be conflicting or out of equilibrium – hence the symbol of the Balance.

The sign of Libra marks the beginning of autumn, which initiates a balance in nature with the falling of the leaves for the formation of fresh humus to replenish the soil depleted by the year's growth. Thus the ground is laid for another spring, just as the Balance phase in man prepares the way for a more complete development through relationships with others; so that man can become aware of his own shadow side and even get to know his own inner partner (which C.G. Jung named the anima for the man and the animus for the woman. See further Chapter 6). In this way, man can reach deeper into himself and contemplate what lies within. This process corresponds to the autumnal period in nature when outer things gradually decay and life returns to the bosom of the earth.

The sign of Libra stands opposite the sign of Aries, that first beginning of the individual when man puts himself in the centre. In the Libra phase, 'the other' is put in the centre and so it is appropriate that it faces the Aries phase – externally anyway. In the Aries phase, growth was internal because the individual took everything on himself; in the Libra phase, growth takes place externally since everything is related to the opposite number and to the part played by the opposite number in the individual's life. What this really refers to, however, is man's relationship with his own inalienable unconscious and it is this that is reflected in the other person. This is a completely new type of experience and it is approached mainly intellectually by the Libra subject; the element air being, as we have said, analogous to the psychological function of thinking. The Libra type will have much to learn emotionally from this first, essential confrontation with another; a confrontation which this type goes to meet cheerfully however, in keeping with the positive direction taken by the energy of the cardinal cross.

A socially conscious relationship with others is important and the Libra subject strives for relationships which are as perfect as possible, and people and situations are compared with and judged by this standard of perfection. This is the stage at which the standards are set and which we shall be expected to abide by in our relationships and social intercourse with others. In this way each can be accorded the recognition and respect due to him on the grounds of his individuality. It is by communication and association with others that our conscious place is objectified.

A person of the Libra types greets social experience with open arms; he has an interest in psychology and in human relations. In his new contacts, he looks above all for fresh knowledge and information to stimulate him mentally – a reaction against the Virgo phase, in which the individual has been putting himself under the microscope, making it imperative for him to turn now to something new outside himself. And so, the person has become an individual who experiences and accepts himself as such; he is not so much concerned with simply functioning in society as in making his individual contribution to it.

Because he thinks objectively, someone of the Libra type can easily put himself in the place of others. On the one hand, this makes him a good diplomat; but, on the other hand, because he sees and understands all points of view, he is quite capable of taking hard decisions or, in another context, is too ready to compromise. He would make an impartial judge, but might find it hard to reach a decision. Irresolution is a characteristic that is part and parcel of the weighing operations of the Balance. The cause here is completely different from that prompting the vacillation of Virgo. In Libra, the hesitation has an intellectual origin, whereas in Virgo it is due to inner uncertainty.

Since the thinking is strongly emphasized and the feeling function is consequently little developed in the first instance, the Libra type is quickly thrown off balance emotionally and fickleness and uncertainty can arise. In the Libra phase, the search for harmony is not so much a native gift as a need supported by such qualities as willingness, friendliness, a degree of enthusiasm and a feeling for aesthetics; while any sentimentality, superficiality and fickleness always emphasize a lack of balance and the incentive for its restoration.

Following the introspection of the Virgo phase comes the intense involvement of Libra with the other world, which is however an involvement with the external form – to which the next sign offers a strong reaction.

Scorpio – the Scorpion

negative quadruplicity: fixed
element: water
day ruler: ☿
night ruler: ♂

After the phase of mainly mental contact on the basis of individuality in the period of the Balance, Scorpio ushers in the phase of emotional experience and of an experiential study of the Libran contacts. The Scorpio phase enables one to experience that making contacts and maintaining relationships are not the be-all and end-all of life and that outward harmony with others is no goal in itself. That is why Scorpio will try to penetrate to the deeper significance of life on earth and to the meaning of human life. Transformation processes at every level in the human psyche are indissolubly bound up with the Scorpio phase. These transformation processes more or less entail that in penetrating the secrets of the human psyche much of personal value must be jettisoned if it is not to inhibit further growth.

In the phase of the Scorpion, autumn is in full swing; the lush external forms have died back to leave nothing but bare trees and bushes above the exhausted earth, and the latter is a carcass from which life can flourish anew. This death in nature is analogous to the crisis suffered by man in the Scorpion phase. Human relationships are expanded and deepened in the form of complete surrender, for example sexually, and in a total use and consumption of self and of the other person – an all-or-nothing approach. The sign is a fixed one and this is an indication here of the tenacity of the sign of the Scorpion; its natives will go to any extreme to retain what they value or what they look on as their ideal. In this respect, the sign shows agreement with the opposite sign, Taurus, which is also very retentive. However, the behaviour of the Scorpio subject is governed not by the desire for material security but by his intense emotional needs. For the water signs, feelings and emotions are the appointed vehicles for growth. In combination with the inner–directed energy of the fixed cross, these feelings and emotions arising from relationships with others are strongly intensified; although this may not be obvious. The element water is introvert and the fixed cross itself is inward looking. The Scorpio subject, therefore, is reserved and inscrutable and both stubborn and passionate. His pronounced inward bias gives him a strong will and great inner strength. People of this type cling so tenaciously to the things they value that they are prepared, if necessary, to pay for them with their lives.

Penetration to the centre of everything and, in particular, to the centre of oneself is the leading theme of the Scorpio type and Scorpio individuals have an unfailing ability to spot the weak points of others. Their uncommunicativeness, their outer control of their feelings, their intense emotional involvement and the way they 'dig deep' prevent them from always being understood or appreciated properly by those around them. Many scarcely suspect what is going on underneath the placid exterior of someone of the Scorpio type.

The depth demanded of one's opposite number in the Scorpion phase means that people at this stage of development become conscious of the partner-image inside them: the anima or female image in the man and the animus or male image in the woman. The deep emotional experience of being reflected in someone of the opposite sex makes it possible to reach down in one's own psyche to its hidden hopes and wishes and to its buried complexes. In contrast to the mental reaction to the partner seen in Libra, the reaction here is emotional, so that a great deal of unconscious material is brought to light. Hence this phase can become one of the really big crises in life and yet, at the same time, one of the most creative and satisfying periods.

In this phase, man is faced with a choice as to whether or not to wallow in his emotions. If he does so, he belongs to what may be called the 'lower' Scorpio type, a type which through its strong emotionality and sexuality and its great tenacity in relationships with others often exhibits a strong possessiveness. The result is often jealous and even violent behaviour or else, where the individual nurses what is felt to be a grievance, his violent feelings are channelled into long-lasting hate. But the individual who does undergo a transformation process in this phase can develop into a 'higher' type, symbolized by the eagle, which can penetrate the secrets of nature quite unselfishly and can delve into the hidden and mysterious on the strength of a feeling which, in a crisis, is transformed from a personal emotional reaction into a precision instrument of pure feeling and sympathy.

Sagittarius – the Archer

positive quadruplicity: mutable
element: fire
day ruler: ♃
night ruler: ♂

During nature's long winter sleep, after the deep enquiry in the phase of the Scorpion, we come to the phase of the Archer, which begins by forming a relationship between external phenomena and the internal experiences known to Scorpio. No longer is the attempt made to fathom the 'whys and wherefores' of things by means of the feelings alone; the search is now made with an abstract spirit too and is aimed at reaching a synthesis. The discriminatory thinking that was characteristic of the previous phases, in which a person's own individuality has been clearly marked out from all others in order to realize his own character the better, now overflows into the need to enjoy something more universal or to discover universal principles. As a fire sign, Sagittarius is mainly involved in intuitive thinking. The empathy with and appreciation of the wider relationships lying behind the facts, sets this phase of the Archer within a bigger framework in which, however, the emotional factor is less than in the preceding phase.

The mutability of the psychic energy indicates that the Archer turns both outwards and inwards at various times; although the impulses which move outward have the upper hand generally speaking, owing to the fact that fire signs are strongly orientated towards the outside world. In this the Sagittarius native is very like Gemini. However, for Gemini the most important thing was the initial contact with the outside world and the task of bringing order to all kinds of things, whereas, in the Sagittarius phase, essential importance is attached to placing these facts and things in a philosophical or religious framework so as to be able to participate in a wider social whole.

The search into the background lying behind appearances carried out in the Scorpio phase is extended in the Sagittarius phase into a search for truth, and the fiery nature of the sign gives a clear indication of the readiness of the Sagittarian to defend his discovered truth with fire and sword; which is why any tact and subtlety are conspicuous by their absence. The idealism of the fire signs may lead in Sagittarius to fanaticism in religion or in some theory of life. Because, in the Sagittarius phase, a start has just been made on arriving at a philosophy of life, the need is felt to become a propagandist. The individual can find a great satisfaction in announcing his new-found truth to others, because this reduces any inner uncertainty he may have. Teaching a doctrine then, is a way for Sagittarius to strengthen his own spiritual basis.

The mutability of the psychic energy in such an outgoing sign as Sagittarius produces a great urge for freedom and travel. After the crisis of the Scorpion phase, the limits of the personal are transcended for the first time. For the Sagittarian, the urge to travel in the sense of crossing boundaries can express itself in concrete fashion in visits to foreign lands and regions or, more abstractly as the study of cultures and philosophies of life. This might be called the search for new inner terrain.

As an intuitive type, Sagittarius always runs the risk of overlooking the personal side of life due to attaching major importance to spiritual laws and ethics. The Sagittarian seeks his goal in expansion and integration and thus combines the fire element with the mobility of his psychic energy. In so doing, he can sacrifice much for the sake of his ideals. His mobility is, however, also indicative of changes of opinion.

Just as in the Aries phase there is a pure manifestation of the individual himself and, in the phase of Leo the second fire sign, the expression of the Ego in all its forms, so in the phase of Sagittarius there is a consciousness of this self, this Ego. The intuitive function type, to which these three signs belong, is represented in the phase of Sagittarius by the man whose insights border on prophecy. The Sagittarian understands that the thoughts and motivations of human beings form civilization and tries to place his own motives in that setting. Thus, in spite of the very personal opinions and subjective 'truths' to which he gives expression, he readily gives an impression of impersonality. A person of the 'lower' Sagittarius type can display a great deal of intolerance together with indiscretion and impatience, but this is a result of unconscious uncertainty towards the newly discovered areas in life. He stands in contrast here to the more evolved Sagittarian who is, admittedly, always searching out the inner side of things but who is also helped by his more universal vision to pay more heed to the opinions of others.

The mutable fire of the Archer produces an attitude which can best be described as filled with hope and even with a childlike and unconcerned faith in the future. Hence, in times of need, he keeps going by being bright and optimistic and by building castles in the air. On the reverse side of the coin, however, this blind trust is attended by a certain amount of danger. Heedless of warnings and full of zeal, he is inclined to ride roughshod over one and all.

The Sagittarian phase is that of the person who feels himself to be part of a greater whole transcending the boundaries of home, family and the local community and, full of enthusiasm, accepts the challenge of finding his own place in that greater whole. This place becomes more definite in the phase of Capricorn.

Capricorn – the Sea-Goat

negative quadruplicity: cardinal
element: earth
day ruler: ♄
night ruler: ♂

In nature, with the arrival of the Capricorn phase, little is left above ground and living things have to prove that they are strong enough to survive the cold of winter. This is analogous to the stage in the development of the human psyche in which everything is assimilated that was learnt and understood about the wider aspects of life in the Sagittarian phase. It was on that basis that a new identity was 'chosen'. In this phase, man has a clearly defined notion of what he is, of what he can do and of what he can achieve within the greater social whole. Stability of form is important to Capricorn as an earth sign and the outgoing energy of the cardinal cross means that someone of the Capricorn type will engage in giving shape to things. So we can regard the Capricorn phase as the highest point of the process in which everything is given form. In the human psyche, this amounts to identification with a certain idea, spiritual or otherwise, while in the social setting the emphasis is laid on the social position as a well-defined whole. Active participation within this whole is no longer one of the aims as it was in the Sagittarian phase where, in the search for the universal principles behind things, no attention was paid to the actual forms under which things presented themselves. In the Capricorn phase, attention is however paid to these forms and the main interest lies in the integration of all of them with particular reference to finding one's own position within the greatest possible whole (such as, for instance, in the integrated unit formed by the state).

A sense of personal prowess is quite considerable in Capricorn but, at the same time, this is the most uncertain factor: it is no more than awareness of a self-chosen identity which have yet to be made good. Here is one of the reasons why it is so important to someone in the Capricorn phase to safeguard his position. As in the other earth signs, the superior psychic function is that of perception and only practical, concrete and efficient methods receive consideration. So then, material security is highly valued, although quite differently from the way in which it was prized as a goal in itself during the Taurean phase. In the phase of Capricorn the need for security stems from a dislike of being dependent that is closely linked with the acquisition of a new-chosen identity.

An individual in the phase of this introvert earth sign, who has to contend with the fact that the way of inner growth is via a clearly mapped inner and outer position, will use his energies in an active manner to achieve this well-planned growth; he will be ambitious and seek status and respect. To this end he will rely on perseverance, thrift, discipline, being business-like, integrity and reliability and, in so doing, frequently give the impression of being rather cold and unfeeling. Nevertheless, a lot is going on behind his unruffled exterior.

Just as in nature there is a struggle to preserve the form which will come to life again in spring, so in the human psyche in the Capricorn phase every effort is made to hold on to forms. Someone of the Capricorn type runs the risk of tying himself up in the strait-jacket of rules and regulations laid down for the benefit of his new-found order and method. The struggle for recognition arising from his urge to preserve the formal side of things can make the Goat lonely and melancholy on his ambitious and upward-striving path in life and this may have repercussions on his emotional experience. It is extremely difficult for somone of a perceptive type like Capricorn to display emotion, since emotion does not belong to the world of tangible and concrete actualities. Accordingly, he will dwell on his feelings for a long time and can find it hard to forget wounding and painful experiences.

Because the Capricorn native is so purposeful, he does not yield to difficulties and is only prepared to give ground if it serves his purpose to do so, regardless of how far in the future his goal may lie. Capricorn patiently endures restrictions, frustrations and difficulties as all these come within the clearly defined framework through which he must pass to his predetermined objective. And so, this phase is an obvious reaction to the foregoing one. The many aims chased by the Archer with such energy have been reduced in the phase of Capricorn to a modest number of practical and achievable long-term goals and the entire life is devoted to making a planned advance towards them.

Aquarius – the Water-bearer

positive quadruplicity: fixed
element: air
day ruler: ♂
night ruler: ♄

The life of nature is still hidden below ground and, after the struggle for survival has centred on the preservation of form in the Capricorn phase, we see in the Aquarian phase how nature finally disposes of her superfluous forms. Everything that has no more use or has not stood the test is given up. Just as the trees let their dead branches fall at this time of year (February is the traditional month for gathering wood!), so, in a psychological sense, the form of the Capricorn phase is broken in the phase of Aquarius. By the use of thought (and Aquarius is an air sign remember) the personal psyche is submitted to an investigation and is analyzed in order to eliminate anything of no use. This means that, as in the Scorpio phase, someone in the phase of Aquarius undergoes a specific crisis; not now over the depths within his own individuality but over the totality of the human condition. The need to penetrate to the universal content of the latter was first clearly felt in the Scorpio phase and is finally satisfied in the period of Aquarius by way of a reaction to the fixity of form prized by Capricorn. This result is due simply to the fact that, in his efforts to break free from forms and to go beyond limits, the Aquarian rises superior to external appearances of things.

The impersonal attitude of Aquarius is a reaction to the strong Ego-sense of Capricorn. The Aquarian can think objectively without consulting his feelings. However, this may mean that he experiences a certain awkwardness in emotional matters. Since his thoughts are so much in control, his love-life is not very emotional – in appearance anyway.

The fact that Aquarius makes part of the fixed

quadruplicity suggests that someone of the Aquarian type absorbs practically all his experiences, including the emotional ones, and 'chews them over'. The in-flowing psychic energy bestows on the Aquarian his great retentiveness of thoughts and ideas. He has advanced beyond their material and external forms but is still liable to be trapped in the thought-forms of his inner world. Owing to his tenacity, a person of the Aquarian type can prove very faithful, even in love, provided he is given the freedom to hob-nob with friends of both sexes. Friendship, the exchange of thoughts and ideas, and love based on similarity of outlook are found at the core of the Aquarian character.

During the Capricorn phase man developed into an individual with a place of his own in the greater social whole and now, in the Aquarian phase, he has become a completely socialized entity who feels most at home when in groups and other social settings. However, the process which leads to the destruction of forms is not directed against collective forms in the first instance but, because the Aquarian refers everything to himself, to the form in which his own individuality manifests itself. For one of the Aquarian type, this 'self-destruction' is indispensable and enables him to place himself within a universal framework and so find himself at the centre of every social relationship. At times he has to contend with a great deal of personal insecurity, which he tries to convert into a feeling of security by expressing himself creatively in a collective context.

His way of breaking through fixed boundaries and forms in reaction to the Capricorn phase makes the Aquarian quite literally a citizen of the world. Nevertheless, the phase of Aquarius is not devoted to destructiveness as such; any breaking down is done with the intention of rebuilding. To return to our analogy, the old branches snap to make way for the new shoots. In this respect, Aquarius is a regenerating and reforming influence. Within the social order, Aquarians are seen as eccentric, unconventional, progressive and resourceful; in spite of the fact that their fixed-cross nature can make them hold so tenaciously to their own unconventional ideas and original thinking that the opinions of others are rejected merely because they are not in agreement with the system of ideas they themselves have constructed – even when the latter is contradicted by the facts.

The less developed Aquarian joins in with as many movements as possible because he blindly identifies himself with the ideals and ideas of the group. In contrast with the solitary eminence of the Capricorn politician, for example, his Aquarian counterpart is more of an egalitarian, and the more evolved Aquarian identifies with humanity at large. On the other hand, because of his arbitrary and unsophisticated identification with some group, a person of the less advanced type can assist in the promotion of factional antagonisms which work against the universalism natural to Aquarius. What we then have is the ruthless revolutionary; the direct opposite of the 'higher' Aquarian, who subscribes to a non-partisan, humanistic and unselfish philosophy of life, based on the mental analysis of what are mainly psychic processes, experiences and events.

Pisces – the Fish

negative quadruplicity: mutable
element: water
day ruler: ♄
night ruler: ♃

Following an encounter with the human condition in a universalist setting, the universal human condition is experienced within the individual personality. This transfer from outer to inner can lead to the eventual return of the personality to the primordial state.

In reaction to the Aquarian emphasis on thought, the experience of the Pisces type is purely emotional. All experiences are very much related to the self but, at the same time, the impersonal element which took shape in the phase of Aquarius retains an influence. Thus the Pisces individual has to face the problem of personalizing all occurrences from an impersonal standpoint, striving to amalgamate the universal human experience with the personality. In its positive form, this attempt is seen as self-denial and compassion and, in its negative form, as a total disintegration of the personality.

In the phase of Aquarius, man becomes master of the process of breaking up old forms in order to build anew. In the phase of Pisces, this breaking-up process is taken to its logical conclusion in the complete destruction of form, so that the individual in this phase can win mastery over what is formless; that is to say, over the world of thought forms. The latter, which can still be a stumbling-block for someone of the Aquarius type, undergoes a transformation in the final phase.

As a water sign, Pisces is very sensitive, often emotional and is very impressionable. Also, as a mutable sign, the Pisces type does not always know what to do with these emotions and consequently falls prey to changes in mood. The psychic energy flows freely and, in Pisces, the battle is begun between personal and impersonal feelings and experiences. It is his impersonal side which makes the native often very easy to influence. This characteristic is especially strong in the less advanced individual to the extent that he is not aware of his own identity and frequently bears the stamp of the person with whom he was last in contact.

The possibility of reaching a measure of self-detachment, which is a property of the mutable cross, reaches its fullest expression in Pisces, the last sign of the zodiac; although this possibility is often beyond the range of vision of a person of the Pisces type. In the first place, his tuning in with others is not conscious and, being governed by the feelings, he has a great capacity for becoming immersed in the thoughts and feelings of others. He therefore has a heightened receptivity to images and diffuse sensations (such as atmospheres created or emitted by others) and this helps to promote a capacity for clairvoyance or other forms of extra-sensory perception.

Due to this susceptibility to atmosphere and impressions behind the more solid parts of reality, the Pisces native tends to have a mystical cast of mind. When the impression endures that there are deeper truths hidden within the external forms of rites and objects, the Pisces individual can become very devout, to the point of slavish adherence to a given doctrine. The great problem in the Pisces stage is the comprehension of the feelings and the uniting of universal human nature with the personal nature. This allows the cycle of experience to continue on a higher plane as the person re-enters the phase of Aries with what has been won in the previous cycle. If the individual is not successful in solving this problem in the development stage of Pisces, it is quite probable that the personality will disintegrate among what C.G. Jung calls the archetypal contents of the psyche. Such an individual becomes a prisoner of ideal imagery or vision and even starts to take on its likeness. In his book *Analytical Psychology* (see *Bibliography*), Jung calls this process the identification of the Ego with the collective psyche. So people of the Pisces type appear to be extremely unstable; an impression which is readily made because, in this stage of psychic development, the individual has already lost essential contact with matter and its forms. These people are rather impractical, prefer to avoid responsibility on this plane, and are happiest when alone with their thoughts. They elect to dwell in their private world of dreams and ideals.

The Pisces type likes to work in large collective organizations, in the background if possible (anonymously and behind closed doors) and where his compassion can express itself in helping others; for example in hospitals and similar institutions.

Owing to the lively movement of his psychic energy, the emotional Pisces individual has considerable powers of assimilation, but these seldom show to advantage because of his lack of self-confidence, which arises from his great emotional sensitivity.

With this, the last sign Pisces, there is a garnering of the final wisdom, the bringing together of all phenomenal forms into a single unity to which the Pisces individual has access as the destroyer of forms and master of the formless. Formlessness contains the total deposit of all the knowledge and experience gained during the whole cycle of the twelve signs but which is bereft of any form which might detract from its universal character of unity. And so, the formlessness which is the end result of the twelve-part cycle and is the germ of a new cycle of experience (commencing in the following Aries phase) will enable the past experience to be tested in practice and to receive additions. The Pisces type, who prepares for the new cycle, can remain unaware of what he is doing, yet nevertheless can mature into an individual who has united within himself the two opposites of the personal and impersonal, leaving behind him, so to speak, a field on which new seed may be cast. In nature too, in the period of the Fish, the ground is ploughed and otherwise prepared for planting and sowing.

6

The Structure of the Houses and the Psychic Structure of the Individual

Synchronicity and Projection

It is one of the peculiarities of our Western culture and of the occidental way of thinking that we locate everything that forms our environment not inside but outside ourselves, and treat events as independent of or 'occasionally dependent on' what is going on in our psyches. In everyday life this shows itself in all kinds of ways, the most important of which are the distinctions drawn between 'good and evil', 'guilty and innocent' etc. This dualistic thinking has found expression in astrology in the dogma that the houses represent circumstances and events which take shape in our environment without our will or conscious intention. It seems as if we are able to exert little or no influence on these circumstances and events and that the only use of the houses is to help us discover what external factors will confront us.

Looked at from the psychological point of view, especially that originated by Carl Jung, a change is made in orthodox notions of causality with the introduction of the age-old formula, 'that which is above is as that which is below' (*quod est superius est sicut quod est inferius*)* in the more accessible, up-dated version known as 'synchronicity'. As already mentioned in Chapter 1 synchronicity offers a meaningful relationship between phenomena without necessitating a 'cause and effect' connection. The principle comes into play where the causal mode of explanation fails to clarify certain happenings. With synchronicity, a new concept as far as the West is concerned, a

*English rendering and the added Latin text taken by translator from Mrs Atwood's authoritative, *A Suggestive Inquiry into the Hermetic Mystery*.
Translator's note.

first approach is made to the a-causal manner of explaining the relationship between oneself and the outside world. The idea is that the circumstances that arise can have a very significant connection with the psychic structure and condition of a person, even though he has not consciously created these circumstances. So it is possible to make the assumption that there is a meaningful link, astrologically speaking, between the houses and the human psyche. This assumption is supported and made more substantial by another psychological concept, i.e. that of the projection mechanism.

There is no psychic life without projection because the projection mechanism is indissolubly bound up with the unconscious part of the psyche. Everything found in the psyche is projected. That is to say that the individual sees in his fellow men and in his environment what he carries in his unconscious self. Carl Jung describes in his *Psychological Types* projection as '... attributing a subjective event to an object ...', so that '... projection is never done, it just happens.' Thus the projection mechanism is an instrument of the psyche which functions entirely outside the will and consciousness. This mechanism can be seen at work most obviously in the strong emotional reactions to people, animals, things and even events. In fact one can project in any direction; the mechanism is not limited to human beings.

Often there is such an extremely strong reaction to certain qualities in others, that it does not matter as far as the projection mechanism is concerned whether the qualities are pleasant or unpleasant. These irrational and emotional reactions are directed against people and things in which we detect such qualities, but what we are really engaging in is a sort of 'recollection' of the contents of our own unconscious. So then, by studying our own reactions to the outside world in the light of the projection mechanism much can be learned about one's own unconscious mind. All the people, things and circumstances with which we feel emotionally involved are therefore tied up with our personal psyche.

Here is where the astrological houses gain new significance. It is no longer the interpretation of circumstances that is important but the understanding of the relationship between these circumstances and the underlying psychological factors

– whether or not the mechanism of projection is involved. In the astrological concept of houses lie both the 'idea' (or 'mental form') as a psychological factor, and the external imposition of form on circumstances, and it should be noted that it is the psychic material which gives shape to the physical material and therefore has priority. The effect of this on the astrological way of thinking is considerable, since one can no longer speak of good and bad houses, since the houses themselves are nothing more than forms of expression of the psychic structure and, as such, no more good than bad, no more conscious than unconscious or, as Jung put it, they are representatives both of the Ego and of its Shadow. They are not so much opposing positions as opposite parts; the separate sections of a single whole – the psyche. But this unit can express itself only in an apparent duality, such as manifests in the human opposites of Man and Woman. Following this line of thought, we can appreciate that in the unconscious of the male his female counterpart is present and that in the unconscious of the female her male part is present, as is so aptly depicted in the ancient Chinese Yin-Yang symbol.

The personality becomes a viable functioning whole when all pairs of 'opposites' have been differentiated and all areas of the psyche, both conscious and unconscious, are interacting. We do not imply that the opposites cancel each other out, that would be to accept the apparent dualism instead of the essential unity. We should think, rather, in terms of pairs which complement each other to make a greater whole. This idea fits in very well with that of tri-unity, an image handed down to us through the centuries as an original component in all cultures and expressed in the astrological house system too.

The Self, the Ego and the Conscious Mind

We may regard what Carl Jung calls the 'Self' as the central point of reference in the many elements composing our psychic structure (see Fig. 6.1). It is a quantity above and beyond the conscious Ego which reaches not only into the conscious part of the psyche but also into its unconscious part. This unconscious presence compensates rather than contrasts with the conscious one; unconscious and conscious are not necessarily in opposition – together they make up the Self. The very fact that the Self incorporates the unconscious part

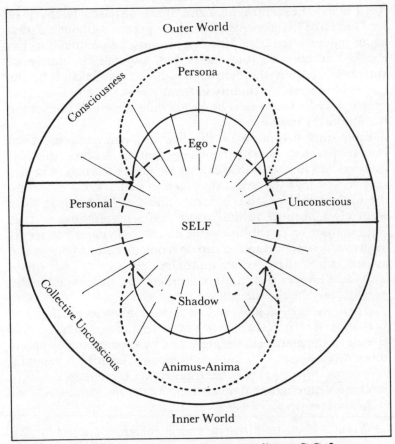

Figure 6.1. The Structure of the Psyche According to C.G. Jung.

of the human psyche means that we can never totally know the Self. We can, however, experience it. The only part of the Self that is knowable for us is the Ego – the conscious part.

The Self is a sort of compensation for the conflict between the internal and the external. It is the purpose of living, for it is the most nearly complete expression of that lottery we call individuality, whether we are talking about separate persons or about a whole group) in which the things mentioned make up a complete picture. The origin of our entire psychic life seems to spring in some inexplicable way out of this 'point' and all the streams that contribute to the highest ultimate goal seem to debouch into it. The Self has been given such names as

'God in us', the 'central fire', the 'spark' (Meister Eckhart) or the 'life force'. It pervades the whole psyche without existing as an independent unit. However, it must be pointed out that the Self is not only the centre but also the circumference surrounding both the conscious and unconscious. It is the centre of the psychic totality in the same way as the Ego is the centre of consciousness. The Self is indivisible and everything is contained within it.

From this definition of the Self as containing the total human psyche, we can conclude that in essence the Self corresponds to the individual horoscope as a whole. For the very reason that the Self is occupied to such a great extent by the unconscious psychic contents and indeed, because 'it is what gives purpose to life as the real representative of that combination of possibilities one terms individual', it seems incorrect to assign it to the sun or moon alone or to one of the houses, since these cover quite limited areas. The whole individual horoscope is most in keeping with the characteristic 'totality' ascribed to the Self.

When we take a look at our individuality in the light of astrology, we find that it is not determined solely by the placing of the planets in the signs and by their mutual aspects; house division too is an important factor. Dane Rudhyar calls the houses the spectrum of the individual experiences.

Human experiences, reflected in the houses, can be related to the universe in three ways:

i) Man is born upon earth and is therefore subject to the laws determined and enforced by earthly life. If we leave out of consideration the form of life on earth, we have here the basis of house division.

ii) Man's birthplace is the solar system. According to the ancient principle, 'that which is above is as that which is below', and also to the principle of synchronicity, man symbolically reflects the heavenly bodies in our solar system. These two factors, astrologically represented in two-dimensional fashion by the planets and houses (or rather, house cusps) in the signs, form the basis of the dispositions and circumstances of the individual.

iii) 'Two brings forth three', says the Tao Teh King (see also Chapter 2), and we observe that a third dimension arises out of two given dimensions. In a material sense we may say that man tries to ensure his place in the universe by learning to control the two basic dimensions. Looking for the third dimension can then be regarded symbolically as what Jung terms the individuation process, the process which refers the Ego back to the Self (i.e. which brings about an interchange between the Ego and the unconscious) so that an individual personality can develop into a universal man.

When we are born, the latitude and longitude of our birthplace (together with the date and time of birth of course) determine our ascendant. This means that we have gained a specific place on earth: we *are*. And thus the first house shows us the birth, the physical embodiment, the natural appearance and the individuality of the native.

However, the mere fact of being here on earth is not enough in itself. Man has an innate drive (in the archetypal sense) to be 'himself', to realize himself and to attain self-awareness. Traditionally, this is expressed in the fire signs. Nicholas de Vore calls the first, fifth and ninth houses the individual or life houses, representing the body, the soul and the spirit respectively.

The inborn drive in man towards self-realization is an obvious fifth house concern within the fire houses. The sun, as Lord of Leo and Mundane Ruler of the fifth house, presents a marked analogy to this drive, which itself shows a close connection with the Ego. Carl Jung defines the Ego as a complex of images which, for the person concerned, forms the centre of his field of consciousness and seems to be possessed of a large part of his inner continuity and identity. We attain consciousness with the Ego because this is the conscious part of the Self. If we regard the sun as the symbol of the Ego, the sun is then the vehicle for the manifestation of the totality of the psyche or Self. The way in which this happens is decided both by the sign in which the sun is posited and by the fifth house. Here we have the external form of manifestation of the Self by means of all kinds of creative impulses and activities. This form of manifestation of psychic drives can have material expression in the procreation of children and the creative production of material things. Enjoyment, recreation and speculation are somewhat less material and even less so are our authority, our will, self-assurance and self-expression; all of which are contained in the fifth house.

In my opinion, the process of evaluating our actions is contained in the ninth house which, according to Nicholas de Vore, is the house of the abstract mind and of intuition, inspiration, dreams and visions. It therefore gives an indication of the native's reactions in regard to philosophy of life, success and religion. In the ninth house we give as it were content to our earthly 'existence' (ascendant) by a process of achieving an awareness through abstract thought and evaluating the way in which we impart shape to our self-expression (fifth house).

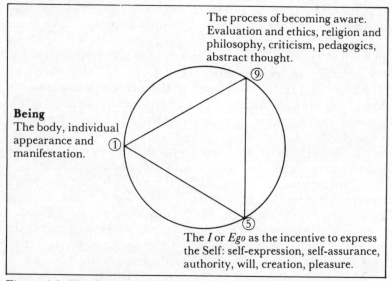

Figure 6.2. The Tri-unity of Life.

The Triangle in Figure 6.2 is not intended to mean that this process of development runs in one direction only, but rather to imply that all three houses are interdependent and supplementary to one another. In outline, Fig. 6.2 amounts to this: houses five and nine cannot function without the physical body (ascendant), and unless he strives to be himself, man cannot grow to be a well-rounded individual. This conscious motivation is inherent in man and should it be lacking, the ninth house would have nothing to think and philosophize about and the body would have no reason for living; there would be nothing for the innate life force or vital spark to express through the conscious Ego. Without evaluation we could not learn from our actions and reactions and what we do and refrain from doing would remain unstructured. There would, therefore, no longer be any question of Self-expression in the fifth house or of individual performance in the first. The individual would turn into a collective being or sort of robot with an instinctive reaction pattern. Thus, if one of the three angles of our triangle were to fail, so would the other two, because they cannot exist without each other. Once more, tri-unity enters astrology.

The idea of 'becoming aware' which belongs to the ninth house must not be confused with the idea of 'consciousness'. Becoming aware is the process involving evaluation and reflection which can help a person to have more insight into himself. This means, in fact, that the person learns to see through his individual form of humanity to the universal character underlying it. This in turn makes it possible for one to consider other individual forms of humanity and collective forms such as cultures and religions which put their stamp on, or form the basis of, our way of life. There is a tie-in here with various notions of mystical awareness which are popular nowadays, and so we are brought back to the concept of Self. Becoming aware in the deepest sense means nothing other than an inner discovery of God and 'coming to oneself' in the fifth house.

Carl Jung took 'consciousness' to be '... the involvement of psychic contents with the Ego in so far as they are experienced by that Ego. Involvements with the Ego which are not experienced as such are unconscious. Consciousness is that function or activity which maintains the relationship between the psychic contents and the Ego.' Therefore it is quite different from the Ego; it filters, so to speak, the information impinging on us from the outside world. It forms the totality of the relationships with which a person identifies himself; which he recognizes and/or remembers and involves with his Ego through the activity of his consciousness. Looked at in another way, it represents our urge towards Self-integration. Accordingly, information coming in from outside is first filtered by the psychic factor in us that we call consciousness before being assimilated by the Ego where it can contribute to Self-knowledge. A certain 'colour' is imparted to this information as it filters through, since complete objectivity is out of the question with a complex psychic structure like ours. However, when one or more complexes create a block for example, we see that in certain instances the consciousness refuses to admit some information. Sham deafness is a well-known example of this behaviour. In such conditions, we obtain not only a highly-coloured picture of the outer world but also (and above all) of ourselves.

If we take the trouble to refer the matters just discussed to the houses, we shall observe that conscious experience can best be assigned to the earth houses. Owing to their emotional bias, the water houses have more in common with the unconscious experience of our psyche (more will be said about this later), and the air houses are (in the words of De Vore) 'relationship or association houses', in which, it is true, the relationships and associations can be made completely consciously, but are derived from the consciousness in the human psyche as such.

From an astrological point of view, the Midheaven shows how we see our formal relationship with the outside world and how we maintain that contact on a social basis as a result. This point (and with it the tenth house) traditionally represents our career, reputation and social position (as a reflection of the manner in which we see ourselves and our attainments in society) – it forms the operational foundation for social intercourse. And so, for the following reasons, we can ascribe the concept of 'consciousness' to the tenth house since our career and reputation largely depend on the way in which we see ourselves and thus on the way in which we are conscious of ourselves. We choose a particular career which, among other things, coincides with how we picture ourselves at that moment. But this can change in the course of social interaction as shown by the MC (i.e. the Midheaven or Medium Coeli) and the tenth house. The Midheaven and the Ego are not identical, because the Ego as such possesses a great deal of internal continuity, which is lacking in the MC or the way in which we relate to the outside world (or see ourselves in relation to the outside world). There is no limit to the way people can chop and change their occupations and their insights into themselves. The MC represents the picture of the Ego with which it identifies for the time being. This means that when it has formed a picture of the Ego, the MC admits only such information as corresponds to the accepted Ego-image. The process can be conscious (e.g. shamming deafness) or unconscious (e.g. the formation of mental blocks by complexes). Hence both the picture we have of ourselves and the picture we have of the outside world are necessarily coloured by the process of selection imposed on all information under the influence of our (temporary) Ego-image as depicted by the tenth house. So planets in the tenth house not only say something about our social careers but also tell us something about how we see ourselves. The manner in which a person looks at himself has a decisive influence on the development of his career.

However, before we know what we identify with, we must go through a process of becoming aware of our pleasant and unpleasant feelings. These are the stimuli for our actions; the fact being that we have to conform to and occupy ourselves with matters with which we would not wish to identify, and this can result in knowledge of and insight into them. The point can be illustrated by means of a simple example. An individual feels restless and unoccupied. He wants something to do and takes a decision as a result of this feeling of dissatisfaction: he decides to learn to skate and starts to take lessons. It leads to a certain amount of proficiency in skating and enables the person to identify consciously with the idea, 'I can skate'. This conscious identification is found in the tenth house, while the longing or dissatisfaction motivating a person to do something are found in the second house, the house of possessions, the house that is analogous to the sign of Taurus. Nicholas de Vore says of the second house that, among other things, it is the place where we encounter the strongest wishes and desires of the individual. Here is the house where one becomes conscious of what one wants and, therefore, we may assign the concept 'personal conscious' to the second house. The financial income and acumen ascribed to the second house are a logical consequence of personal consciousness. Those conscious feelings of longing or dissatisfaction are a spur to action. Such action when taken can lead to skills and accomplishments capable of serving as a source of income.

The term 'personal' implies that in no case need the wishes and desires be of universal application. They may even come into conflict with what is generally wished and expected – by the collective conscious. The collective conscious is a factor in our psyche with which we do not identify; nor does it have a direct action on our feelings of pleasure or otherwise. Carl Jung understands by this concept '... the totality of the traditions, conventions, customs, prejudices, rules and standards of human collectivity, which give direction to the consciousness of a group as a whole and are unreflectingly observed by the group members.' In part, the concept covers that of the Freudian Super-Ego but differs from it to the extent that Jung understands by it, not only the 'introjected' commands and prohibitions of the external world springing back from inner psychic space, but also the commands and prohibitions which continually govern the person from outside in what he does and refrains from doing and in his feelings and thoughts. Introjection is a mechanism opposed to projection, and means the assimilation of the object in the subject; in other words, it is the experience of factors lying outside the psyche as if they came from within. Because we do not identify ourselves with it directly, the collective conscious serves as a frame of reference for the personal conscious. As soon as the contents of the personal conscious deviate too widely from those of the collective conscious, this will lead after a certain time to an internal and/or external conflict impelling us to make better use of our feelings of pleasure or otherwise and to tailor our Ego-image to fit reality. The sixth house, analogous to Virgo, is the house that represents this function within our psyche. If we do not have an accurate idea of what we can do and suffer (in consequence of our feelings of liking and dislike as shown by the second house) and we go out into the world with a false idea of ourselves (tenth house), we shall meet the much-needed counter-reactions which should put us right. For example, if we are an employee, we might get a reprimand from the boss (sixth house!), or we might become unwell because, psychologically, we are no longer able to bear the circumstances arising out of our false Ego-image. Illness due to stress from assuming too much responsibility or from having too many irons in the fire in general, is a corrective factor. Sickness, like employment belongs to the sixth house.

In this, the earth triangle or tri-unity, too, (Fig. 6.3) it is clear that no one factor can be taken apart from the rest without upsetting the balance. Without the personal conscious there is no possibility of identification on a conscious level and the comparison can no longer be made with the contrasting collective conscious. Without the collective conscious no one could really become conscious, because there would be no standard of comparison. In that event, all that could be said of the individual would be that he *is*. Growth into a genuine state of consciousness would fall by the wayside.

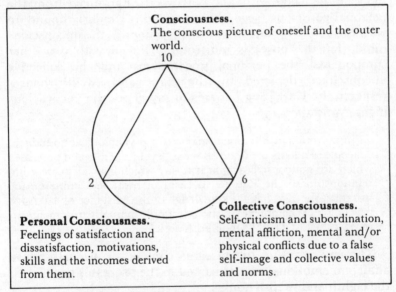

Consciousness.
The conscious picture of oneself and the outer world.
10

2   6

Collective Consciousness.
Self-criticism and subordination, mental affliction, mental and/or physical conflicts due to a false self-image and collective values and norms.

Personal Consciousness.
Feelings of satisfaction and dissatisfaction, motivations, skills and the incomes derived from them.

Figure 6.3. The Tri-unity of Consciousness.

The Unconscious, the Persona and the Animus/Anima

As opposed to the conscious mind, the unconscious mind does not reveal itself in thinking and reasoning but in the feelings; feelings that almost defy analysis simply because they do arise out of the unconscious. Carl Jung says that compensation is a typical characteristic of the unconscious (which normally represents the customary external reactions of the individual to a given situation) by a typical reaction derived from human experience and obedient to internal laws.' Dr Jolande Jacobi adds the comment that compensation allows an individual to adopt an attitude in keeping with his whole psyche.

The opposites, conscious and unconscious, are expressed astrologically in the opposing fourth and tenth houses. It is the fourth house that we find the above-mentioned reaction derived from human experience that surfaces from time to time, in for example, a feeling for tradition, a sensitivity to 'atmosphere' and in the basic emotional attitude of the individual. In this house lie those reactions, arising from the inner depths of the psyche, for which no rational explanation can be offered.

Just as the conscious mind in the tenth house forms an indissoluble whole with, and borrows the Ego-image from, the personal conscious (second house) and is similarly bound up with the collective unconscious (sixth house), the unconscious mind (fourth house) is indissolubly linked with two other components: the personal unconscious and the collective unconscious, depicted by the eight and twelfth houses respectively. Carl Jung has this to say about the unconscious in his *Psychological Types*:

> ... in my opinion, the unconscious is a psychological boundary-concept used to incorporate all those psychic factors and processes which are not conscious, that is to say which bear no perceptible relationship to the Ego ... in cases of hysterical amnesia, for instance, the Ego has no knowledge of the existence of extensive psychological complexes, although simple hypnotic treatment can recover the lost data at a moment's notice.

The emergence of unconscious contents is a fourth-house affair; an emotional matter rooted in the processes peculiar to the eighth and twelfth houses.

The collective part of the unconscious contains, not those contents which are specific for the individual Ego or come from personal experience, but those contents resulting from the inherited possibility of the activity of the psychic functions, i.e. of the activity arising from the inherited brain structure. According to Carl Jung this inherited brain structure is generally human, perhaps even generally animal-like, and it forms the basis of all the individual psychic behaviour. The unconscious is senior to the conscious; it is the original factor from which the individual consciousness must emerge. The collective unconscious consists of the deposit left behind by the psychic reactions of humanity from the very beginning – with no reference to historical, ethical or other differences – in general human situations, e.g. in situations involving fear or danger, in struggles against superior numbers, in sexual relations, in the relationship between children and their mothers and children and their fathers in particular, in behaviour influenced by love and hate, by birth and death and by the principle of light and darkness, etc. All these things comprise what Jung terms archetypes, primeval images which lie at the basis of all human psyches on earth and offer an explanation for the striking similarity between the images and contents of mythologies and fairy-tales in all cultures (see also Chapter 1 on this point).

The archetypes play an important rôle as formative influences in the psychic process and are expressed in a specific manner for the individual in dreams, associations etc. The manner and measure in which they play a consciously perceived part in our life is definitely linked with the twelfth house.

The personal unconscious holds contents which have a bearing on the life history of the individual. It holds elements that have been repressed, forgotten or perceived subliminally (that is to say just below the threshold of consciousness) and also everything that is unconsciously sensed, felt or thought. The personal unconscious is not merely the reservoir of all sorts of things we no longer wish to know and therefore repress; it can also store matters of which we are still unconscious. This accords with the possibility of transformation traditionally ascribed to the eighth house.

The feelings obtained via the fourth house influence can be assimilated and admitted to consciousness, but there is also the possibility that certain feelings are too much for the individual and are then driven back into his personal unconscious. He may behave as if there were nothing to worry about and, for a long time, quite successfully too. However, the more experiences of this sort that are stored up, the more the eighth house exerts its influence by way of 'complex forming'. A complex is a psychic force which, at times, puts the conscious aim and freedom of the Ego completely out of play. In this connection it should be remarked that a complex ought not to be designated as good or bad; it is a sign of uncombined or unassimilated psychic contents. These unassimilated contents can be a hindrance but, at the same time, they can provide an increased incentive to get things done, for the simple reason that more psychic energy is concentrated in them. Thus complexes can make a contribution to success in life.

To begin with, a complex expresses itself quite harmlessly in slips of the tongue or pen and in forgetfulness. If complex formation in the eighth house goes further and the first small warnings are ignored, the warnings become more serious and compelling while what Jolande Jacobi calls the functional disturbance centre increases in size. Eventually, this centre can encroach on the collective unconscious and there bring certain achetypes to life with the result that the total unconscious behaves more and more compulsively. As we have already seen, the unconscious is a compensation for the conscious part of the psyche. This means that just as our conscious actions and modes of thought diverge further from our Self and thus from what we are in the depths of our being, so the unconscious contents gradually come 'more into the open' and force abnormalities on the conscious part of our psyche. When this process is noticed in good time by the person concerned, he can go to a psychiatrist for treatment (eighth house); if his condition deteriorates and he loses control of his conscious mind, he will have to be admitted to a mental hospital (twelfth house). Nevertheless, the unconscious can play a creative rôle of great importance. Archetypal factors and symbols can be merged with contents in the personal unconscious which are not connected with repression mechanisms, and can therefore have a very creative effect (eighth house).

A balance is then struck in the feelings and emotions which emerge in the fourth house. This means that the fourth house is the result of the unconscious processes; what for want of a better word I call the 'Unconscious'. (Fig. 6.4).

The fourth house may be considered the tip of the iceberg of the unconscious as a whole (Fig. 6.5); a whole in which there is a living interaction between the different layers of the unconscious.

The conscious part of our identification with our Ego (the

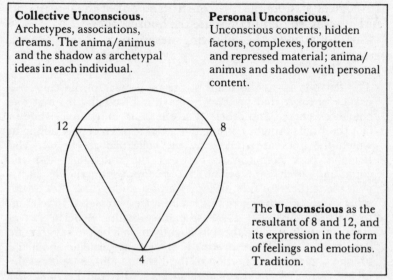

Collective Unconscious.
Archetypes, associations, dreams. The anima/animus and the shadow as archetypal ideas in each individual.

Personal Unconscious.
Unconscious contents, hidden factors, complexes, forgotten and repressed material; anima/animus and shadow with personal content.

The **Unconscious** as the resultant of 8 and 12, and its expression in the form of feelings and emotions. Tradition.

Figure 6.4. The Tri-unity of the Unconscious.

MC and tenth house) is connected with the unconscious fourth house, which forms the necessary (unconscious) psychic counterpart of our conscious processes. However, both houses are bound up with each other in another way. In the case just mentioned, their relationship is complementary and compensatory; they work as a team. But when we take a closer look at the concept 'persona', we realize that from the

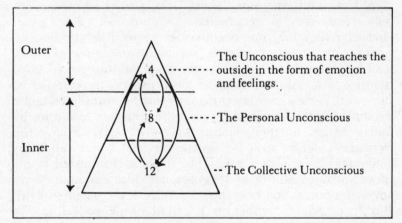

Figure 6.5. The Interaction Between the Layers of the Unconscious.

astrological standpoint it is constructed out of the fourth and tenth houses, so that in this case the houses 'agree'.

Carl Jung gives the following description of the concept persona:

> The Persona is, as the name suggests, a mask of the collective psyche, a mask that pretends to have individuality, so that one convinces oneself and others that one is an individual, while in fact the whole thing is nothing but a clever piece of play-acting in which the lines are spoken by the collective psyche. ... The Persona is a compromise between the individual and the community over how a person should conduct himself. He has his own name, bears a title, occupies a post and is this, that or the other. To a certain degree this is all perfectly real, but in relation to his individuality it has a secondary reality, being a sort of compromise in which others frequently have a bigger say than he does himself. ... There is already something peculiar about the unique choice and definition of the Persona and, in spite of the identification of the Ego-consciousness with the Persona, the unconscious Self, the specific individuality, remains in existence and is directly as well as indirectly observable.

Taking our cue from the above, we can place the compromise between the individual and the community as such in the tenth house without hesitation. However, the way we conduct ourselves and the attitude or mask we adopt are also in great measure dependant on our emotional life and its associated complexes and emotions. There belong to the Persona not only our mental characteristics but all our social characteristics too; our peculiarities as seen by the outside world, among which Jolande Jacobi mentions our posture, walk, clothing, 'tics', usual laugh, etc. From the psychlogical point of view, all these external forms express the complexes, present to a greater or lesser extent, which lie concealed in the person's unconscious and, as we have seen, are found in the fourth house. So then, on the MC − IC axis we have the Persona; man's socially acceptable behaviour and his customary style − or mask. This disguise is adjusted to his inner and outer worlds and it guarantees him a comparatively smooth, natural and easy intercourse with the outside world. But the protective 'rubber mask' can fit a little too well so that the face behind it is squeezed into a permanently fixed expression. Only the individual horoscope will show whether and to what degree this is so.

The more we identify ourselves with our mask or Persona, the more the following happens. In the first place, we extend the range of things with which rightly or wrongly we can or will identify in attitudes, ideals, profession, etc. Conscious identification becomes more marked and the logical consequence is that our unconscious counterpart also increases in strength and range and throws more weight into the balance (the fourth and tenth houses always form the Persona *together* without working against each other). Jung has this to say about such an increase in the importance of the Persona: '... all factors which do not fit into this whole are disowned, forgotten or overlooked, or even completely repressed.' The agreement with the selective action of the Midheaven could scarcely be closer. 'But too much has to be sacrificed for the sake of the ideal image on which one would like to mould oneself,' continues Jung, 'that is why "personalities" are always over-sensitive, for something can so easily happen that makes them aware of an unwanted facet of their real (individual) character.'

If we further elaborate the rôle of the Persona, we come up against the concepts of the Anima (for the man) and the Animus (for the woman). Carl Jung represents the relationship between the Anima and the Persona in the man as follows (for the Animus the corresponding situation is true):

> ... the lack of resistance to the influence of the Persona points to a corresponding inner weakness in regard to the influence of the unconscious; feelings and moods, anxiety and even a feminine type of sexuality (to the extent of impotence in the extreme case) come more and more to the fore. The Persona, the ideal image of the man, with which he identifies and to which, in his own eyes, he corresponds, is internally compensated by 'feminine' weakness. When the individual plays the 'tough guy' on the outside, he becomes feminine on the inside in his Anima, for then it is the Anima that opposes the Persona.

In astrological terms, this complex set-up is no longer contained within the MC – IC axis alone. On further analysis of the question of Persona versus Anima, the other earth and water houses have to be taken into account.

The Anima (and the Animus too, but I shall limit myself to a consideration of the male psyche here for the sake of convenience) is the unconscious counterpart of the feelings of conscious personal pleasure or discomfort, and therefore belongs to the eighth house. The Anima is in essence the 'inner woman' of the man: his feminine image. He is entirely unaware of the existence of this image and projects it on the woman with whom he is in love, regardless of whether she really meets its requirements or not. He simply 'sees' it in her. Being in love with another is really being in love with one's own unconscious in its capacity as the counterpart of the conscious. So being in love can provide each of us with an important key opening a door to self-discovery. This is an eight-house matter, but unfortunately it usually stops at the stage of a temporary narrowing of consciousness; something we can also place in the eighth house.

These processes are illustrated diagrammatically in Fig. 6.6. Through his feelings of pleasure or discomfort, an individual learns to build up a picture of himself with which he identifies. In other words he moves from the second to the tenth house. The more strongly he identifies with the conscious part of his persona, the more energy he 'invests' in his tenth house and MC, and the more intensely the unconscious part of his psyche will operate (in the fourth house, which is fed by the contents of the personal unconscious). The Anima, which is assigned to the eighth house, influences the feelings of the fourth house along an unconscious route and in such a way that this fourth house acts in a compensatory manner towards the strong conscious identification with his ideal self-image. Houses four and ten, the Persona, keep each other in balance in the ideal case, but oppose one another in action. The same is true of houses two and eight: the personal conscious and the personal unconscious. The stronger our own distinctive wishes and longings become (second house), the greater becomes the force with which repressed contents from the eighth house obtrude themselves on the fourth house and with which Anima (or Animus) and Shadow generate unconscious feelings and desires.

The Shadow in us is our mysterious doppel-ganger, the

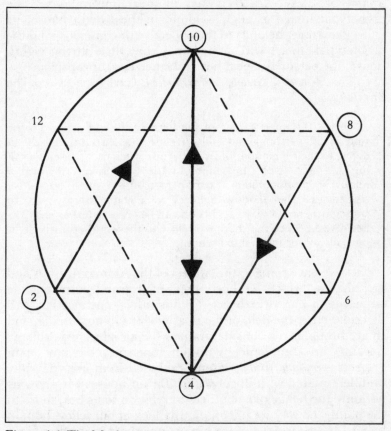

Figure 6.6. The Mechanism Associated with the Persona-axis.

counterpart of that part of us with which we identify ourselves; the double which, recognized in another person, provokes our spite or simply compels admiration, because we are still unaware of its presence in ourselves. We become aware of this Shadow only when we see through the mechanism of projection and can use others, on whom we project our own shadows, as mirrors. In this respect it might seem to be rather like the Anima/Animus. However, the Shadow, our 'other private personality', is of the same sex, whereas the Anima/Animus image is of the opposite sex. In the dreams of a man, the Shadow will step forward in the person of a man, while the anima will be a woman. Both archetypes are tucked away in our unconscious. The archetypal image as such is found in the twelfth house; its collective aspect belongs to the collective unconscious, and the archtetypal image with a personal content is in the eighth house; the personal aspect lies in the personal unconscious.

In his *Memories, Dreams and Reflections* Carl Jung says of the Shadow:

> ... this is the inferior part of the personality and makes up the sum of all personal and collective psychic dispositions which, owing to their incompatibility with the consciously chosen way of life, are not 'lived' and unite in the unconscious to form a relatively autonomous semi-personality with oppositive tendencies. The Shadow behaves in a compensatory way to consciousness, therefore its action can be positive just as easily as negative ... Since the shadow is close to the world of instincts, it must always be taken into account.

Now we have come to the subject of the Anima/Animus and the Shadow which we encounter in projected form outside ourselves in our sweetheart, friends, idols, enemies etc. We therefore enter the field of the relationships in human life, and so are brought to a consideration of the air signs of astrology. Because, in compliance with an inner psychic law, man projects *everything* that is latent, excluded from everyday life, undifferentiated with unconscious, the air houses will show us not only the behaviour of others in relation to us but, more to the point, the way we unconsciously look at our fellow human beings. In this way what we project on others in the first place is reflected back from them. The implication is that we project our own unconscious good and evil characteristics on others but believe these characteristics to be in them. Since this projection mechanism is an unconscious one, we *think* that the fault lies in the other person whereas it really lies deep within ourselves. People tend to commit themselves to those whose characteristics agree with or are similar to those of their own unconscious minds.

The initial contact, the superficial acquaintance, the first experience of the given duality, belong to the third house. In this house we become aware that the other person calls himself 'I' too and so distinguishes himself from us. The psychic behaviour peculiar to this house is paying attention, communication and the exchange of information, in addition to the experiencing of the immediate environment and of the duality it contains with regard to oneself. The third house represents both the form in which the so-called 'brief encounters' take place and also our own inner attitude to these encounters.

The actual interaction between ourselves and others, that is to say our living and working with them, is found in the seventh house. This is where our opposite number manifests as a partner in all senses of the word. Planets in this house represent not only certain qualities in the partner but, in particular, what we project on the partner and unconsciously expect of him or her – even to the extent of bringing out the projected properties in the partner. The seventh house, which is situated opposite the first, or our own Being, stands for the Being of the 'other' both in fact and in our own psyche.

Exactly as the third house (being aware of others) lies opposite the ninth house (being conscious of oneself) and the seventh house (the Being of the 'other' person) lies opposite the first house (one's own Being), so the last air house, the eleventh, lies opposite the fifth house (the house of our own self-expression). This eleventh house represents the self-expression of others, of the group, of society perhaps, at least as we experience it; it represents teamwork in associations, clubs etc. Internally, this house shows the degree to which we can or will participate in the 'inner group' to which we feel related and in which we abandon group setting. It is not for nothing that it stands opposite the fifth house!

In the same way that our Mask or Persona can be found in the horoscope, we can also derive our individuality from it. The first house is where the individual appears. This is a primary appearance with no extraneous colouring and no 'taking thought'. In the seventh house we saw our unconscious, equally primary reaction to the presence of the 'other' (but remember, becoming aware of that 'other' is a third-house feature). This 'other' seems mainly to derive his or her value from projections of our own unconscious, so that the seventh house represents the primary reactions to our own inner nature, whereas in the first house we saw a primary reaction to our exterior. There is no hint of a mask in these two houses, all we have is an elementary state of being.

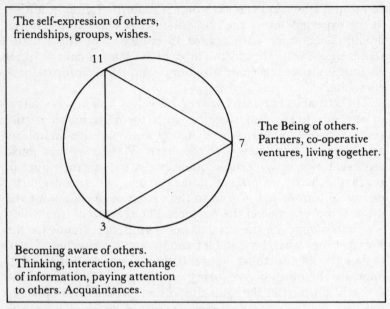

The self-expression of others, friendships, groups, wishes.

11

The Being of others. Partners, co-operative ventures, living together.

7

3

Becoming aware of others. Thinking, interaction, exchange of information, paying attention to others. Acquaintances.

Figure 6.7. The Tri-unity of Relationships.

Our individuality expresses itself by means of the fifth house. This is self-expression, but we recall our own individuality only in the process of seeing ourselves reflected in others. In that way we can penetrate our own unconscious minds, can get to grips with our own individuality and can grow up into individuals in Jung's sense of the word. However, *all* the houses are needed for this achievement, as illustrated diagrammatically in Fig. 6.8.

As this Figure clearly shows, there is a conflict between our Individuality and our Persona: the two axes cross one another at right angles. It is the integration of the two axes, with the help of all the houses or, if you will, areas of our psyche, which can bring us closer to our Self, to our true nature. For this purpose, our psyche has at its disposal various instruments that act as pairs of opposites:

1 – 7 axis: the personal Being versus the Being of others;
2 – 8 axis: the personal conscious versus the personal unconscious;
3 – 9 axis: becoming aware of the other person versus becoming aware of oneself;

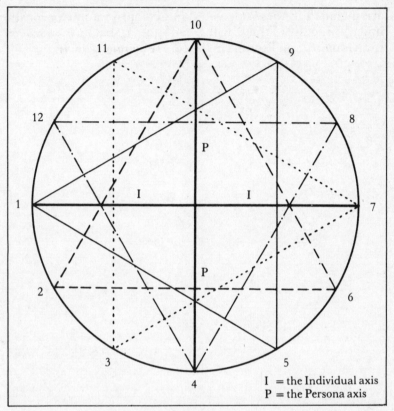

Figure 6.8 The Persona and the Individuality Axes in Relation to the Four Tri-unities.

4 – 10 axis: the unconscious versus the conscious (what is meant here is the eventually openly-expressed result of the two tri-unities of which they form part).

5 – 11 axis: the personal self-expression versus the self-expression of others;

6 – 12 axis: the collective conscious versus the collective unconscious.

When we learn to differentiate all pairs of opposites, which are really contrasting halves, and learn to bring about a living interaction between the conscious and unconscious parts of our psyche, we are then in a position to develop into a true individual. The others and the other, our whole circle in fact, are included in these opposites and comprise a mirror for the inner processes that will lead to a balance between Individuality and Persona in the course of inner growth.

7

Planets as Symbols of Archetypal Psychic Drives

Introduction

> Behind the pleasant façade of consciousness with its disciplined moral order and its good intentions, there are hidden primitive instinctive life forces like monsters of the deep – devouring, voracious and for ever on the war path. It is only rarely that we get a glimpse of them and yet life itself is borne along by their urgency and energy. Without them, living beings would be as immovable as blocks of stone.
>
> M.E. Harding

When man began to spread abroad in the early days of development, his psyche was much involved in the struggle for existence. The pioneers were kept busy defending themselves against other forms of life, in looking for food to keep body and soul together and in procreation to preserve the race. As a consequence of these biological preoccupations the human psyche developed certain types of reaction and behaviour patterns in the course of time. These were, so to speak, stored up in the collective unconscious of humanity and, in the shape of archetypal factors, they continue to play a part in the human psyche right down to the present day. It was pointed out in Chapter 1 that Carl Jung regarded archtypes as the regulating principles in the unconscious part of the human psyche and that this material lying in the collective unconscious is every bit as much inherited as our physical characteristics are. We see that, as the human potential further unfolds, the range of experience widens and the archetypcal contents of the collective unconscious increase in similar measure. As a result of the multiplicity of experience encountered by mankind in the course of centuries upon centuries, there is a great variety of patterns of instinctive behaviour. These inherited unconscious behaviour patterns are the drives behind present human activities and, for the astrologer, they are symbolized by the planets.

Nevertheless the life of man would be on an animal level if it were conducted solely on the basis of these instinctive and unconscious impulses. But consciousness arose from the ocean of the unconscious and man began to build a community life which became the basis of the civilizations and cultures that flowered later. As manners are refined and human consciousness grows, the fight for physical existence as such loses its dominant rôle. Individual self-defence is exchanged for partial responsibility for the defence of the community, and the uncertainty of the food supply, is overcome by human ingenuity. Now, however, there is a struggle imposed on the individual owing to the rift betweel cultural and psychological values on the one hand and purely biological drives from the unconscious part of the psyche on the other hand.

Quite unconsciously, man tries to channel a number of his natural impulses and to divert the energy associated with them to other goals. Through the conflict between unconscious forces and conscious tendencies and the inevitable creation of a culture to cope with it (a culture which makes necessary finely-developed codes of conduct) new experiences are repeatedly added to the human collective unconscious. The altered reaction-habits brought about in this way and the further extension of patterns of behaviour already adopted not only have given a more differentiated content to the archetypal images already present but have also created new ones down through the centuries. Looking at it in this light, it is not so strange that from time to time new planets are discovered: always, when in the course of human development completely new conditions arise, new archetypal images will also arise in the human psyche by the transformation of existing patterns. If credence is given to synchronicity (the meaningful relationship of events having no causal connection), it is certainly not unthinkable that the discovery or observation of a material phenomenon should be synchronous with and analogous to a new archetypal arrival among the psychic contents. For example, in 1781 the planet Uranus was discovered during the prelude to the French Revolution, which had far-reaching results in large parts of

Europe. Astrologically, this planet is the symbol of the impulse towards renewal and individual freedom. It was at this period that the idea of freedom and independence was enshrined in the Constitution of the United States of America (signed in 1787); the independence of the United States had been won shortly before in the struggle for freedom from the Motherland, England, which was compelled to recognize the independence of America after a decisive defeat in 1781; a recognition ratified by the Treaty of Versailles in 1783.

In the history of humanity as a whole, developments take place in a way which would have been unknown or impossible at an earlier date. Their occurrence is the result of the totality of the inner psychic developments in man as an individual. Whenever this inner evolution of man becomes a new psychic fact and the said developments have found their place as archetypal images in the human collective unconscious, then a fresh pattern of instinctive behaviour emerges from the existing patterns; a pattern which, on the basis of synchronicity, can be symbolized by a newly discovered planet.

The transformation of primitive instincts is an important process in human development. Thus, it can be established that the instinctive sensation of hunger, which is a purely biological urge for the sustenance of the body, is gradually converted into an instrument of the conscious ego. Thus it is no longer an isolated impulse restricted to satisfying the pangs of hunger but also becomes an impulse towards the satisfying of the psychic needs of the conscious Ego. Hence ambitious behaviour can develop, in the form of either the tendency to acquire possessions or the cultivation of status. In a further development of this basic impulse, personal limitations can be transcended, and then the chief motive is no longer to increase the Ego's good opinion of itself. A religious or other altruistic ideal becomes the goal of the hunger-impulse energy. However, the fact that the two other possibilities for channelling psychic energy (as described above) remain present in the human psyche, even when the conscious goals are unselfish, becomes obvious when the 'threshold of consciousness' is lowered. So then, it is possible that someone who seems to be totally in command of himself in all circumstances will suddenly act aggressively under the influence of tensions, drink or other problems, and to a degree that no one would have expected of him. In this case, it is the latent instinctive behaviour patterns in the collective unconscious which may make themselves felt. Thus a person who, in normal times, has a reputation for sterling honesty, can turn out to be a cunning thief in times of famine and the survival instinct emerges in its most elementary form.

In a social sense, each instinctive behaviour pattern has its positive and its negative sides. But while the instinct for survival can make a thief, it can also make a statesman of the man who outgrows his ambitions. We see, therefore, that each planet has several sides to it as far as these instinctive behaviour patterns are concerned, and can express itself on different levels. It is extremely important not to look blindly at the external appearance in psychological astrology but to try and see what patterns can underlie the multiplicity of apparently unconnected forms of expression and behaviour. Just as a thief's impulse to steal and the ambition of the great statesman may be traced back to the instinct for survival, so can planets (to which the next section of this chapter will be devoted) display totally different and sometimes apparently opposite effects which nevertheless have a common cause.

According to the psychology of Carl Jung, there is stored in the collective unconscious of the human psyche the whole of man's experiential knowledge and patterns of behaviour. An account of this theory has already been given. Each individual is alleged to share in that store and, from an astrological point of view, we may add that *all* that is contained in the planets, when they are treated as symbols of these primitive patterns, is present in every horoscope. And so, we all have *everything* belonging to the planets in our horoscopes or psyches (whichever way you look at it), but the specific pattern formed by the planets in the natal horoscope reveals how various planets play a part in the life of the individual. What is shown, in other words, is those patterns of instinctive behaviour which are most accessible to the individual. The psyche is a complex whole; nothing in it functions independently, everything is interconnected. This is strictly true of the planets in a horoscope too. There are numerous possibilities for relationships between the planets, such as aspects, rulerships etc. Therefore no single planet can be interpreted as an isolated element; the whole horoscope must always be taken into consideration in determining the rôle filled in the psyche by each factor. And, within that total picture, the astrologer must allow for the three stages of development of instinctive behaviour inherent in each planet. At present, it is impossible to say which stage of development in instinctive behaviour will apply in a given horoscope. If we could do so, we could invariably tell the difference between the horoscope of a man and an ape say.

M.E. Harding calls the first stage in the development of an instinct (analogous to that of consciousness) the naïve stage, in which life is lived unconditionally at the behest of purely biological needs and impulses. The second stage is the Ego stage in which consciousness awakes with the Ego at its centre and so the instinctive drives undergo a transformation. For example, man is able to resist hunger and appetite if doing so will serve certain ends. In the final stage, it is possible to integrate the energy of the instincts in what Carl Jung has named the Self. The conscious Ego is experienced as relative in this stage; it is experienced merely as one part of the total psyche and therefore as subordinate to it. The Self, on the other hand, is the centre of the total psyche and includes its conscious and unconscious parts at one and the same time. The religious mystic is inclined to speak of 'seeking God in oneself' when he means searching for the Self.

There are three different stages of consciousness which more or less form part of the human psyche. One can never be in only one stage. M.E. Harding writes: 'The business of everyday living would scarcely be possible if one were totally liberated from the needs of the body or had totally discarded one's Ego wishes. These drives belong to the human condition and without them there would be an end to the life of the body and to that of the conscious personality.' In addition, it is worth noting that the Mahayana Buddhists also distinguish three stages of consciousness and that these are in remarkably close agreement with modern Western psychology. To put it briefly, these three stages amount to the following:

i) The naïve stage or the stage of the 'person with little understanding, as the Mahayana Buddhists put it. In this stage, human consciousness is very limited and is restricted to physical needs and wants;

ii) the Ego stage or the stage of the 'person with normal understanding'. Such a person has gained a certain amount of control over his instinctive drives. The Ego is now the deciding factor, and everything is marshalled in accordance with its own values. According to these values, whatever the Ego regards as good is accepted and whatever it regards as bad is rejected. What the individual at this stage fails to realize is that the many rejected factors accumulate in the unconscious, from which they can broadcast messages that tend to 'jam' those sent out by the Ego. All the energies are devoted to satisfying the demands of the Ego;

iii) the stage of the Self, or of the 'person of superior understanding'. In this stage, identification with the Ego is abandoned to make way for experience of the inner world as a dynamic factor. The Mahayana Buddhists say, in this connection, that the best thing that can happen to someone is for him to become absorbed in the deep inner realization that the knower, the known and the act of knowing are inseparable. Unity is the central point of all.

In each of the three stages, the psychic energy bound up with the primitive drives of man is differently applied and so has different results. Some indication of this has already been given in the remarks on the instinctive satisfaction of the hunger sensations. A great deal depends on the degree to which the individual himself can transform his psychic energy. As little as it is possible to talk of good or bad energies, so is it hardly possible to talk of good or bad planets as the representatives of certain energies. There are planets with certain conceptual contents and aspects representing specific energies, but it depends on the conscious attitude whether these are experienced as good or evil. So then, an unpleasant experience cannot only teach a person how it may be avoided in future but may also help him to cope better with other eventualities. What is evil at one time can be good in altered circumstances. It is very hard to draw the dividing line between one and the other when life is experienced as a flowing stream of events.

Thus certain planets, such as Saturn, which are described

as malefic in traditional astrology, are in fact the cause of any number of possibilities, but the experience we draw from them simultaneously offers us the chance to delve deeper into our own psyches and frustrations, to track down our hidden complexes and, in so doing, to make a fresh start. An individual in the naïve stage of consciousness will see himself confronted by insuperable difficulties and feel frustrated in his attempts to satisfy his inclinations. Someone in the Ego stage will find himself frustrated because something is holding him back from the attainment of whatever he wishes to identify with, and he will rail against what he regards as fate or the opposition of others. The man in the stage of the Self seizes the inhibiting experience as an opportunity to follow some fresh path to the goal that inspires him; he also looks for a clue that will give him an insight into the cause of the original restriction. Feelings of fear, inhibition and limitation will also be proportionally less than in the previous stages owing to the relatively lesser importance of the Ego.

It is extremely difficult to tell from a horoscope at which level the energy of the archetypal contents of the collective unconscious part of the psyche are going to manifest. This means that we must be satisfied for the time being with the knowledge that these levels do exist. But even if we could discover rules which would give us some indication regarding levels, it would still be a critical matter interpreting them. For although we have been considering three distinct stages in the development of the conscious mind, it goes without saying that there is an infinite number of intermediate possibilities. And so, the concept of 'stages' or 'levels' becomes even less comprehensible. What then is the point we are trying to make? From what has been said in previous chapters we can conclude that we shall have to look for the frame of reference within our own psyches and not in our Egos or conscious minds alone. Metaphorically speaking, we can never avoid viewing ourselves and the things around us through coloured spectacles. How then can we assess exactly what is the colour of the spectacles through which someone else is looking – in accordance with the stage he has reached? Even the wish to be as objective as possible has inescapable subjective overtones: we operate with our total psyche and this is organized in its own special way. We look through the glasses of our conscious

and unconscious values, wishes, longings, opinions and so on.
The desire to be objective is something that as conscious
identification comes under the Ego image.

But even in regard to the content of astrological concepts
over which we can reach mutual agreement, we do not escape
from the colouring this content has for us. Even in the most
cautious interpretation, a value-judgement is unavoidable
either in the choice of words or 'reading between the lines'.
We can never know to what extent someone else understands
the same thing as we do by the terms used. Although we
employ the same words, the thought world behind them
differs from person to person, and this all too often gives rise to
misunderstanding and verbal strife. Incidentally, the *mot* that
the interpretation of a horoscope reveals more about the
interpreter than it does about the native, is as much applicable
to the interpretation of the horoscope of a primitive warrior as
it is to that of a conscientious scholar. Both are inevitably
bound up with their own psyches and with the colourings
peculiar to them.

The stages of development of the conscious mind and of the
instinctive behaviour discussed here must not therefore be
thought of in terms of better and worse; they merely represent
a line of development. All three levels have their advantages
and their disadvantages and, for this reason, the three
different levels cannot be separated when one is thinking
about the planets. Both the constructive and the destructive
modes of expression have to be given and can be considered as
advantages and disadvantages at all three levels.

Planets, their positions and their aspects are energy
patterns, and the use of this energy creates certain results
through the Law of Cause and Effect; results which take the
form of developments within the human psyche and
happenings outside the individual in the world around him.
Obviously, someone living in the naïve stage will have less
comprehension of the results of his dealings because he is
unable to take the broader view possible at the Ego stage in
which one gains a certain amount of foresight.

In this connection, it can be remarked that the traditionally
'good' placement of a planet in its own sign says little about
levels. This optimal placement simply tells us that the
characteristics of the planet concerned (or, to look at it

another way, the given primeval contents of the psyche) can reach maximum expression and deployment both destructively and constructively. The possibility of anticipating results and/or of gaining insight into the consequences of one's own actions is not implied by this optimal placement. A natal horoscope can be identical with the horoscope for the moment when the first foundation stone of a house is laid. In the horoscope for the house there is no question of determining levels of psychic development; at most one is concerned with whether or not the whole edifice is well founded. In the human horoscope the placements and aspects of the planets and the like show what sort of foundation for life is present and what are the possibilities for building further on this specific foundation.

The Classical Planets

Sun

In modern astrology, which is grounded in astrology, the sun is often seen as a symbol of the Self, and so as the most important part of the horoscope. (See Jeff Mayo: *The Planets and Human Behaviour*. Details in *Bibliography*). In the sense given to it by Carl Jung however, the Self means much more than can be expressed by the sun. The sun is one of the archetypal patterns in the human psyche. It is a very important pattern, certainly, but in no case does the sun include both the total unconscious and the total consciousness of the human psyche. It has already been suggested, in the previous chapter, that the concept of 'Self' seems to be most in harmony with the total horoscope.

On the analogy of the sun as the centre around which everything else in the solar system circles, the sun in the horoscope forms the centre of the conscious part of the psyche: the Ego. The Ego is the central reference point with which every other factor in the horoscope has to be connected (a requirement which does not necessarily imply that the sun must have many aspects). It represents the innate impulse each person has to be themselves, to realize themselves and to achieve self-awareness. Although each individual is cast in a unique mould, there are twelve basic patterns discernable, symbolized by the placement of the sun in the twelve signs of the zodiac. This placement shows how he will attempt to realize his aims and ideals, how his Ego will respond to situations and events and how he will organize his complex whole to deal with possibilities. These actions and reactions flow from an archetypal compulsion, either in the form of unconscious motivations or as the much more conscious result of thoughts and ponderings. However both are expressions of the same archetypal content of the Ego in the psyche.

The sign in which the sun is placed reveals the deepest nature of an individual, but this need not mean that he will express himself in the manner characteristic of that sign. The sun symbolizes the path pursued (in this case the path of individuation), and the sign occupied by the sun shows the way in which this path can best be followed. Hence every sign is as much good as bad and none is superior or inferior to any other.

Essentially, the sun is concerned with the manner in which a person may achieve harmony with himself or, to put it in psychological terms, with the way in which the totality of the personality can be realized. At the same time, the sun has a mainly integrating function for the conscious part of the psyche, which Jeff Mayo has expressed as follows in his definition of the sun: '... the attainment of unity and uniqueness by means of the integration of the diverse components of the psyche in such a way that each component can function at its best as an integral part of the whole.' The various components of the psyche can be interpreted in an astrological sense as the diverse parts of the horoscope, and then the above quotation can be taken to mean that, by following the pathway indicated by his sun, a person is in a position to integrate the other parts of his horoscope, however incompatible they may be. For just as the planets would not show up in the blackness of space without the illumination of the sun, so we can become conscious of our other planetary factors only through the function of the horoscopic sun.

As far as the earth is concerned, the sun is nothing less than its source of energy, the maintainer of life itself. In a horoscope, too, the sun signifies life force, creative power, warmth, vitality, dynamism, creativity and vigour. The person who comprehends the psychic contents of the sun (which amounts to being and understanding himself) is in a position to develop characteristics ascribable to a constructive use of the sun, and which are in keeping with the sign of Leo ruled by the sun. These characteristics include self-confidence, will-power, purposefulness, independence, generosity, loyalty, dignity, creativity and charismatic leadership. The impulse towards self-realization can express itself in ambition and a desire for power, manifesting in such destructive forms as ruthless power complexes, egotism and egocentricity, boasting and putting on airs and graces, and despotic behaviour. It is also possible that a negative activation of the sun will lead to timidity, incompetence, a lack of self-reliance and a lack of ambition.

The integrating function of the sun assumes the presence of organizing and controlling abilities such as have been ascribed to the sun (and to Leo) from time immemorial. Organizing, controlling and integrating the conscious part of the psyche are the functions symbol the sun is the symbol in the horoscope.

Moon

Just as the astronomical moon is visible from the earth in her perpetually changing phases, so the astrological Luna is also a 'fluctuating' principle. She is symbolic of the realization of the life process begun by the sun. The sun is the conscious Ego of man from which the moon, as the representative of unconscious emotional behaviour and of unconsciously acquired actions, derives light, for the moon is a reflector. Viewed psychologically, the one stands for 'being onself' while the others stands for 'doing what is expected of one'; in other words it is the Ego versus the Persona or mask (see Chapter 6). The moon indicates the unconscious, conditioned emotional behaviour of man; his way of reacting and doing things which stem from wholly unconscious drives, when he does what feels good without bothering to think about it. To a great extent, education and inculcated, socially acceptable behaviour form the background of the 'self-evident' reactions of the moon, both in the most concrete form of bearing children and in the abstract form of reproducing what has been learnt or experienced.

As the representative of the conscious Ego, the sun has as its opposite number the moon, representing the unconscious, and in this sense the sun could hardly manage without the moon. Astrologically speaking, she rules over a great variety of things on earth. One primeval force lies at the basis of everything. There are almost as many names for the force as there are religions and philosophies, but it is the moon that wields this primeval creative principle and, by virtue of her reproductive capacity, manifold phenomenal forms make their appearance. The moon gives shape to the creative impulse from the sun. Those properties in the horoscope that are peculiar to the sun can be activated only in collaboration with the moon, which confers form on the life processes. The conscious and unconscious parts of the psyche can unify that psyche only by concerted action, and the conscious Ego of man can hold its own only when the archetypal contents of the unconscious support the processes of the Ego. If they do not do so, it becomes subject to irrevocable breakdown and/or change.

The moon's links with the unconscious part of the psyche make her contents available to the symbolizing faculty of the unconscious. Under the moon come all forms of fantasy and imagination. Used constructively, they add up to creativity, but if they are used destructively the person concerned is too easily influenced and unreliable.

Just as a person can adjust to his environment consciously through the psychic factors represented by his sun, so he is bound to his environment in ways he does not realize by those represented by the moon, which often exert a great influence on his emotions and frame of mind. And just as the moon in the sky proceeds changeably through her phases, so changeable are the feelings and affections of man, and the more so the stronger is the influence of the moon (and of Cancer its associated sign) in the horoscope. The changes of mood initiated by the moon are like the constant ebb and flow of the tides and they make a similar impression of restlessness on others.

Sensitivity, fancy, susceptibility to impressions and feelings, reflection and adaptability are lunar factors in the horoscope which go hand in hand with the things already mentioned. Constructive assimilation of the psychic contents symbolized by the moon gives, in addition to the above characteristics, sympathy, productivity, tenacity and prudence (prompted by the inclination to stick to the tried and trusted) and a good memory. The retention of impressions and especially of emotionally charged events, is a typically lunar characteristic. As ruler of Cancer, Luna is bound up with tradition, the past and feelings, not forgetting the need to take care of, mother and protect someone. When the moon is strongly placed in the horoscope, these things are often much in evidence.

An inferior placement of the moon can encourage traits in the way of instability and unreliable behaviour, changeability, restlessness, favouritism towards one's own family and the adoption of prejudiced opinions. Since the moon takes no initiative by itself but simply gives shape to whatever is communicated by the rest of the psyche, a negatively emphasized moon can indicate a weak will, apathetic behaviour and a tendency to indulge in emotional outbursts.

As the symbol of unconscious, conditioned emotional behaviour, the moon can (as already seen) express itself in different manners which, at first sight, appear to have little in common. However, the great unifying factor is the fact that the lunar attributes have so many roots in the human unconsciousness. To sum up, the psychic contents symbolized by the moon make their appearance as:

- reproductive capacity, both in knowledge and, on the material plane, in the form of motherhood; giving form to the impulse emerging from within, just as that luminary reflects the light of the sun;
- emotional factors: the reaction of the unconscious to events taking place in the environment; fluctuating feelings analogous to the lunar phases;
- a combination of both the foregoing, i.e. the reproduction of what is learned and the reaction to the tried and trusted can produce a ready opportunity for feigned behaviour – the mask of Persona.

Mercury

'The resources of the human psyche and its essential nature are very probably determined by the instinct to think and reflect.' So says Carl Jung and M.E. Harding comments:

In consequence of this urge or need to consider experiences, to be able to summon them before the mind's eye again and to transmit them to others, the primitive instincts in man (and in no other living creature) have been liable to a certain degree of change and have, to some extent, been deprived of their involuntary effect. They have gradually become subservient to the needs of the psyche instead of remaining irrevocably bound to the needs of the non-psyche, that is to say of animal life.

Thinking, reflecting, analyzing and exchanging ideas are processes ascribed to Mercury by traditional astrology and treated by modern psychology as the expression of an instinctive behaviour pattern that, like all other archetypal factors, is present in each one of us. This neutral and combining planet apparently plays a more important rôle in the human psyche than is usually perceived. It is clear from the above statements by Jung and Harding that without the psychic contents of which Mercury is the symbol, man would be nothing more than a mindless and purely instinctive being. Liz Greene is right in saying that Mercury, '... is the great reconciler but equally the great destroyer. Through his power to divide, discriminate and sort out, the individual can become aware of underlying relationships between things or, on the other hand, he may become alienated from these relationships by indulging in the collection of isolated and meaningless data.

The planet Mercury stands for the way in which man assimilates his experiences and factual findings and the way in which he thinks and communicates his thoughts. The hermaphroditism (or double nature)* of Mercury, seen in his inner side (thinking) and his outward form (communication and exchange) and so clearly expressed by M.E. Harding, agrees in every respect with his rulership over the introvert, analytical and meditative sign Virgo and over the extrovert, contact-seeking sign Gemini with its facility for liaison-work.

In itself, the drive is neutral in character and non-emotional; though, of course, emotions derived from other psychic contents may lend it a certain colour. In principle, the central feature is the linking of facts and factors. The process which brings about and maintains communications and exchange makes these factors indispensable for the process of

*Words in brackets added for clarification. *Translator's note.*

becoming aware. Mercury motivates the integration of unconscious drives through conscious recognition and for this reason the presence of the sun and moon can be made even more obvious. When these two are not consciously analyzed and combined (analysis and reflection are conscious processes), they can make little contribution to the personal psychic development due to a lack of insight into actions and impulses. Particular emphasis is laid here on the conscious area of the psyche because, by definition, the unconscious part is unknowable, and man must use his conscious part to try and understand himself and, in doing so, to gain insight into his 'other, darker side'. A neutral analysis of conduct and motivation is therefore indispensable or, to express it astrologically, Mercury's influence is absolutely essential. Now if a man could not see himself reflected in others and if he could not compare himself with them, there would be no such thing as consciousness; only by experiencing differences from the outer world and changes in time can man comprehend what he is and what he is not and, in doing so, gain an insight into who he is. Therefore, the exchange of experiences, ideas and analyses (Mercury's external form) is essential. It is that part of the human psyche which not only joins the inner being and the mask together, but also provides for their connection with the external world.

As, in their purest form, thinking and analyzing are intellectual processes (they are diametrically opposite to feeling), Mercury also symbolizes the need to store up knowledge and information for later use in communication, whether this process is carried out by gesture, word of mouth or writing.

The Mercury factor can express itself constructively in man as great analytical skill, eloquence, desire for knowledge and mental adaptability to the latest insights and theories. The more destructive side of Mercury in man is seen in a hypercritical attitude, cunning (due to the emphasis laid on the seeing of less acceptable possibilities in social life), fickleness, unreliability and loquacity.

The mobility of Mercural thinking, when Mercury is strongly emphasized in the horoscope, are indicative of restlessness and quick-wittedness in debate, while a less well placed Mercury promotes such things as forgetfulness and irritability. The ability to make connections and to see all sorts of possibilities inclines the person with a strongly emphasized Mercury to display irresolution. He attaches equal weight to all sides of every question. Furthermore, a certain measure of nervousness is a feature of a strong Mercury factor.

To sum up, Mercury as a linking entity, or the urge to think, analyze and exchange information, plays the following part in the human psyche – and therefore in the horoscope:

- reflection on experiences and facts in as objective a manner as possible, in order to marshal data;
- forming connections between carefully arranged data and theories in order to gain insight;
- exchanging and changing thoughts over individual findings;
- analyzing differences on the basis of the findings of others;
- reconsidering and arranging the view obtained in order to reach newer insights;
- making connections between all facets of the psyche, both conscious and unconscious. This creates the possibility of integrating these factors.

The way in which all this happens depends on the sign occupied by the planet Mercury. The thought processes need not be strictly logical in themselves. Reality and the world can be experienced in all kinds of ways and they can be classified and linked up in mental constructs in many ways too. All the sign does is to show how the individual experiences and how he categorizes the phenomenal world mentally. It is the process itself that belongs to the Mercury factor in the psyche, the further content is determined by contacts with other planets.

Venus

The male and female part of the psyche is represented in an astrological sense by the symbols of the sun and moon; the psychic factor of Mercury makes it possible for a person to experience this (both inner and outer) duality and to remember it, reflect on it and place it in a framework of relationships. An urge to unite opposites, to harmonize and bring into equilibrium is the essence of the next psychic factor, symbolized by the planet Venus. The mental evaluation of what we experience takes place through the function of Mercury and the emotional side of what we experience is evaluated by the Venus function.

An important rôle is played, in particular, by identifying oneself with certain values, whether they be internal or group values. Harding writes: 'The instinct for self-preservation,' (to which we may relate the planets Venus and Mars) '... has had a very important positive effect on society, because it has promoted mutual relations between people. Obviously, the lives of individuals are best protected when people unite in groups and offer each other a helping hand. Friendships easily develop in such groups ...' In big groups like this values and forms of behaviour are produced so as to create solidarity and give coherence. Taking the signs in order, we may observe that this occurs in the phase of Libra, ruled by Venus. Readiness to compromise plays a big part in friendships and group relationships and this is a function typical of Venus.

The psychic contents of Venus have developed to more abstract forms with man himself, starting with the simple need for human togetherness and resulting in friendships and the various forms of living one with another. And so we have the evaluation of perceptions and experiences on the basis of the feelings; although the function of Mercury is necessary to put them into words, to exchange opinions on them and compare them. We also have, in Venus, the entering into relationships on the basis of mutual dependence, the maintenance of balance and harmony in relations by mutual respect and recognition, and the already mentioned uniting of opposites, by which the Venus function becomes the power source behind expressions of love and affection.

Co-operation and partnership, harmony and balance, sympathy and humanity, idealism and peaceablness, artistry, aesthetic sense and a feeling for beauty are all characteristic of the Venus function. But when the psychic function symbolized by Venus is disturbed, a lack of readiness to co-operate comes to the fore, together with disorderliness, clumsiness, lack of tact and living by standards considered immoral by the group.

Consciously joining in with others was necessary not merely

for self-defence but also for the preservation of the species. Although, strictly speaking, the moon has most connection with motherhood, the relationship with a partner and sexual intercourse (symbolized by Venus and Mars respectively) precede pregnancy. In this context, Mars stands for the desire and Venus for the wish and need to be desired. So Venus is linked with the ability to appreciate one's own power of attraction and with the accompanying feeling of vanity. An unbalanced Venus function in the psyche can, by over-emphasis, lead to excessive vanity or, by under-emphasis, to self-effacement and the feeling that the individual's desirability and attractiveness are insufficient and that he is a failure. Both overvaluation of oneself and overcompensation consequent on undervaluation of oneself can produce the dandy and the prima donna. The apparent effects are the same in both cases but the underlying causes are completely different.

Generally speaking, the urge to enter into engagements springs from the need for security. Early in the history of the human race, this led in the naïve stage to the combined effort in foraging for food and in mutual defence, and these things contributed to physical security. In the ego stage, this archetypal factor in the psyche developed into a need for personal security by ensuring the presence of a life partner or the like. This development from the collective to the personal has found abstract expression in the need to collect things of beauty as a means of security; in this form there is a clear influence of Venus in Taurus. Both partner and things are readily seen as a possession and a source of security. The psychic contents symbolized by the planet Venus also represent the impulse to assign values to objects, persons and situations, chiefly on the basis of feelings. These values can prove decisive in the personal sphere for our feelings of pleasure or dissatisfaction (the Taurus factor in the human psyche). On the interpersonal level the said values can shape society (the Libra factor). The emotional relationships are important here; mental relationships lie more within the province of Mercury, religious relationships within that of Jupiter and eventual form within that of that demarcator of boundaries, Saturn.

Mars

The aggressive form in which the instinct for self-preservation occurs is symbolized by the planet Mars. We seldom see a complete identification of the individual with the values adopted by the group (Venus) and so there are wide individual differences. Those who deviate too much from the collective norms often represent a source of tension and conflicts. The more they deviate the more the individuality is emphasized and the more the pressure to conform is exerted by the group. In the human psyche, Mars represents the first impulse to hold one's own against others. In no way, however, does this mean that someone with Mars prominent in his or her horoscope is sufficiently advanced to be himself or herself or, as Carl Jung would say, is well on the way to individuation. Mars is more likely to find expression in the urge to prove oneself, to demonstrate that one is a 'somebody' and to hold one's ground at all costs. M.E. Harding notes that 'The aggressive instinct seems to be exceptionally difficult to transform, perhaps because (in contrast to the hunger impulse) it necessarily employs primitive means to attain its ends. A person who eats needs not infringe the rights of another, but a fight, even in self-defence, involves the use of aggressive as well as protective mechanisms.' Hence the Mars contents of the psyche can alienate an individual from his group, which is held together by Venus factors (representing in this instance the opposite influence) that can afford him security.

Alienation from the group need not be seen as directly negative. Mars is the motivator and the beginning of the actions which, by means of the self-defence mechanism, can help the individual create the possibility within himself to break free from parental and family ties. This first attempt at 'proving oneself' can develop to the point where the Uranus function joins forces with the Mars function, and the person, guided by an inner sense of destiny, creates his own values from the contents of his psyche.

Nevertheless, in many instances the Mars function of man makes no direct contribution to inner refinement; its power of action, energy and self-assertion, ambition, aggression and pugnacity are pressed into service in the struggle against others. Although the Mars factor has little to do with the emotional life of man, it can arouse many emotions. Feelings of pleasure and dissatisfaction play a big part here, though in a quite other sense than in the Venus factor. The individual is so closely involved with his sense of individuality. Mars symbolizes the strong personal involvement in what is experienced; whether the experiences lie in simple initiatives or in the sexual field, everything is felt most intensely. As ruler of Aries, this planet also gives the fierceness, the undirected energy and the sense of adventure characteristic of the person who feels sure of his place in a group but, at the same time, is inclined to behave like a separate entity because he is not dependent on the group as an individual. The clash between acceptance of the group's protection and resentment at the restrictions imposed by it gives rise, understandably enough, to bouts of self-assertion and generally aggressive behaviour.

Where the Mars factors are expressed constructively, the character is conspicuous for its independence, courage and enterprise, love of action and pioneering spirit, together with great spontaneity. His highly competitive spirit and determination to win are factors which help the individual on his way up the social ladder. On the other hand, when the Mars function is difficult, courage can degenerate into recklessness, the urge towards self-expression becomes impertinent, wayward and egocentric, while aggression and assertiveness can turn into bad temper, destructiveness, pugnacity, rudeness, violence and ambition of power. Impulsiveness can develop into impatience and intolerance and, in short, the uncontrolled and fiery power for Mars, the aggressive expression of the instinct for self-preservation, can all too easily have serious consequences for the individual when there is nothing indicated in the horoscope that would mitigate it. Presumably this is the reason why, in previous centuries, this planet was looked on as so strongly negative and 'malefic'. Its ardour can break things up and obviously, years ago, there was far less tolerance of any infractions of accepted norms and values than there is in modern society. However, there is nothing 'bad' about the psychic contents of Mars in themselves. Mars shows us the way in which a person establishes himself, conducts his activities and experiences his sexuality, and also (according to the placement in sign and

house) where he is deficient in the Mars characteristics
mentioned. It is an indispensable function of the psyche to
break free of the current and customary group conventions in
order to operate as an individual within a group. In view of its
aggressive side the Mars function prepares the way for
someone in a collective setting to take the first individual steps
on the path that will lead him to 'becoming himself'.

Jupiter

The statement was made right at the beginning of this chapter
that in the course of human development there began a
transformation process of instinctive impulses, by which the
instinctive mechanisms of the human psyche were made
subject to the modifying influence of moral, social and
religious factors. Man abandoned the purely impulsive
approach, his activities came increasingly under conscious
control, so that the automatic character of instinctive
behaviour has been partly lost. A new archetypal idea has
taken root in the human psyche, manifesting itself in an
impulse which we encounter only in man, the spiritual and
religious impulse. Carl Jung comments, '... the spiritual
propensity also appears in the psyche as an urge, indeed as a
genuine passion. It is no derivative from some other drive, but
a principle *sui generis*, that is to say the form in which the
motivating force must manifest.' By 'drive' or 'urge' he means
impulsive action, that is to say functioning without a
conscious motive for doing so.

It is this spiritual and religious need of humanity which is
represented by the planet Jupiter. This impulsive psychic
factor puts the impulsive factors discussed earlier in a broader
perspective, creates the possibility of channelling the psychic
energy bound up with them and, in essence, is the first step in
the direction of their conscious realization. At the same time
there is an expansion of the archetypal ideas connected with
each of the impulsive factors. So the survival instinct, which is
revealed, for example, in the purely biological faculty of
hunger, becomes further differentiated on the psychic level,
where its parallel in hunger for knowledge becomes a driving
force behind the ambitious behaviour of various individuals.
The Jupiter factor in the human psyche represents the driving

force behind this type of extension of the primitive instinct. Thus extension and expansion are part and parcel of Jupiter. Growth of awareness and insight, and an increase in knowledge and understanding, are all Jupiter matters enabling an individual to conduct his primitive urges along more sensible pathways.

The impulsive factors represented by Jupiter itself have also undergone changes in the course of time with this broadening of the psychic contents. When people began to come together in groups for the sake of mutual support and safety, the standards and values which were adopted held the group together. These were welded into a social system under the influence of the spiritual basis, and faith, together with its dogmas, rituals, taboos and codes of conduct, formed the chief means of channelling the aggressive drives (Mars). The functions of head of state and high priest were often combined in one person. The emperor in ancient China, the Dalai Lama of Tibet, the pharaoh of Egypt, were all seen as the direct representatives or descendants of God. In a later development, when the theocratic form of government had been abandoned and the gap between 'church' and 'state' widened, Jupiter became more associated with obedience to internal standards and laws, and inner religious experience took the place of collective experience. The principle of growth and expansion inherent in the energy mirrored by Jupiter is also applicable, therefore, to this impulsive expression of self.

Jupiter relates to everything that tends to increase or extend, and therefore to propulsive and motivating instinctive forces which give the psyche its boundless energy. The expansion of awareness by means of knowledge and study has already been mentioned, but material and physical expansion (literally in the sense of corpulence) also come under Jupiter. A need to explore the possibilities of the material, mental and spiritual skills latent in one's own constitution is accompanied by the need to disseminate the insights acquired so that others may share them. The improvement or, properly speaking, the expansion of one's own character on the mental and emotional plane and the improvement of one's own social position are mainly guided by the conscience. This is because the Jupiter factor in the psyche is answerable only to the conscience and an innate sense of fair play. What we are saying amounts to this: nobility, generosity, justice, piety, magnanimity and the instinct to heal and protect are the conspicuous traits of people in whom the Jupiter function is pronounced. When this function is expressed less constructively, however, the expansive tendency is either restricted or else overemphasized. Helpfulness can turn into intrusion, and obedience to an inner voice can result in outward lawlessness, self-righteousness and conceit. What is more, characteristics such as a compulsive desire to rise to the top, overrating one's abilities, rashness, prodigality and hypocrisy can make their appearance. The desire to broaden one's own knowledge and understanding and then to promote whatever is found to be of value can, in this case, easily become fanaticism and a blind adherence to, and defence of, chosen dogmas. Instead of furthering and deepening insight, the Jupiter factor can then do the reverse and assist the spread of misconceptions, so that the individual withdraws from any possibility of increased awareness.

Growth and expansion is also a feature of the Jupiter impulse itself. Hand in hand with the religious thirst for an experience of the unity of all things within oneself, goes the need for a deeper life and an enlargement of the experiential and environmental world. This is the root of the longing to know and participate in whatever lies beyond the horizon, both literally and figuratively. Voyages and journeys from country to country and from one philosophical or religious scheme to another, afford the opportunity of understanding one's own world better and of seeing the relativity of things in the light of the added experience and knowledge gained. Tolerance can also result, and matters can be seen in a wider context. The desire to discover what is beyond the horizon is also expressed in the wish to overstep the boundaries of today and view what is held by the morrow. Prophets and seers are traditionally associated with Jupiter, which has actually been called the planet of wisdom.

Because of the insights obtained, this particular psychic factor is also linked with the capacity for forming judgements. This puts a person in a position to take part in life in a more balanced manner and to conduct himself more thoughtfully. Here too we see that, when the Jupiter impulse is used injudiciously, optimism can lead to recklessness; so that someone with a poor sense of judgement (i.e. someone who fails to make constructive use of the archetypal Jupiter function in his psyche) can lose everything he has so painfully built up in one big gamble. By such an experience, which owing to its painful nature belongs to the following planet, Saturn, the individual concerned can learn to appreciate things differently and then the principle of expansion of awareness proper to Jupiter will develop in a new way.

Saturn

During the early development of communities, religious taboos and social regulations restricted the natural instinctive reactions of man, but individuals accepted this pressure out of necessity. It was only through these regulations that community life, which was the basis of secure existence in regard to safety and food supply, could continue. The emergence of social standards (Venus) and of religious virtues and commandments (Jupiter) lies within the instinctive pattern of the human psyche. M.E. Harding observes that with further social development,

> ... one instinct came to be set against the other and the one kept the other under control, giving rise to a conflict between desires and given objectives. Consciousness was enhanced by this conflict, since the individual had to make a choice if he did not wish to abandon himself to indecision with destruction as its outcome.

So man was faced with the decision to suppress his aggressive impulses (Mars) or to sublimate them in some way, to ensure his place in the community; a decision which had to be taken consciously in the presence of the many instinctive inclinations which continually rose up within him. It was his unconscious self that both supported and threatened him and his only salvation from the constantly conflicting unconscious impulses was the formation of a consciousness which would make it possible for him to make his own decisions about himself, instead of allowing himself to be tossed to and fro by his urges. 'Consciousness only arises because of discomfort', says M.E. Harding.

Growth in consciousness is associated with withdrawal of

psychic energy from the instinctive drives in order to apply it consciously to given goals, and from this a centre of consciousness develops in the psyche, namely the Ego, which has the ability to see itself – to a certain degree in each instance – in relation to the rest of the world. And so it is the Ego which eventually emerges out of the unconscious of the human psyche. Carl Jung talks of an Ego-complex that is formed and that precedes the formation of a conscious Ego.

From an astrological point of view, the conscious Ego comes under the Sun, whereas the clash between the instinctive drives in the human psyche and the learning process which accompanies them is symbolized by the planet Saturn. The Saturn function in the human psyche represents much more the process of forming the conscious Ego than it does the conscious Ego itself (= the sun). Through the formation of the conscious Ego, man can no longer ascribe all his unconscious motivations to incredibly powerful beings and spirits outside himself; he is forced to recognize the consequences of his actions and is made to learn how he can influence 'fate' by making use of what he has learnt from experience. He has slowly learnt to know and recognize the law of cause and effect, so that strict rules are no longer necessary for regulating society from without (such as religious laws for example) as there has been a development of moral sense and conscience. Both the (internal and external) moral order and conscience have been ascribed from antiquity to the planet Saturn.

Perseverance is a part of this psychic factor for '… although the Ego-complex arises spontaneously, it has to be made conscious through sustained and directed effort, if it is not going to remain in a primitive and elementary state. Without this, no further psychological development is possible.' It is noteworthy how the traditional meaning of the planet Saturn agrees with what the psychology of Carl Jung ascribes to the process of developing the Ego. M.E. Harding puts this as follows:

> The development of the Ego brings with it certain positive values of great significance both to the achievement of maturity by the individual and to the accomplishment of some task in the world. Self-respect is one of the most important of these values. To this we can add ambition in the positive sense, expressing itself in the

desire to do good works, to get on in the world, to play a fitting rôle, not only out of considerations of prestige but in order to satisfy one's own inner standards. These qualities are connected with the sense of being a personalized Ego; an 'I' with rights and dignity, someone who is a worthy member of society and able to hold his own, even when the support of society is withheld from him.

The inwardly sensed need to participate in society demands a concentration of energy on the chosen goal and a large measure of tenacity. This tenacity and the urge to consolidate creates the inner strength to work towards a certain goal over a long period of time and to rise in the world. (Jupiter is responsible for the extended working hours and Saturn is responsible for the hard effort!) The psychic factors symbolized by the planet Saturn take shape externally in the rules and regulations enshrining given social virtues in various forms.

An increasing amount of psychic energy is liberated as the Ego develops. This energy is withdrawn from the instinctive drives and is made available to the conscious mind. As already pointed out, the latter can use it for attaining the self-appointed goals and for fulfilling wishes and desires. However, a concentration of energy directed towards some goal requires regulation and control; structural boundaries and fixed limitations are necessary to prevent a leakage of energy. In this respect, Saturn signifies the individual's need to demarcate, limit, restrict and give shape to his goal-consciousness, for the sole purpose of constructing a realistic and practical life-style on the basis of solid material values. The ambition inherent in this factor is accompanied by a sense of responsibility and obligation: man is no longer content to blame what happens on intangible entities such as demons and spirits.

The development of a conscious Ego is a process in which man arrives at an increasingly clear picture of himself and the outside world through the constant conscious learning and comparison of data and experience. Man acquires wisdom by falls and recoveries, and this is typical of Saturn's characterization as 'learning through pain'. The properties of sobriety, loyalty, introspection, fear, retirement, pessimism and patience, traditionally ascribed to Saturn, are quite understandable in the light of what has been said. The learning process is part and parcel of unpleasant experiences, by which grief, trouble, care, feelings of guilt, adversity, coldness, delay and even death are connected up with this psychic factor. However, by learning from these frustrations and restrictions, a person is placed in the position to arrange his life better and, by deeper self-knowledge, to gain more self-trust.

The anxiety involved in relinquishing an old form imparts a certain degree of inertia. Because of the conflicting factors in the psyche it becomes necessary from time to time to abandon or alter conscious identifications (see also Chapter 6). The process that must lead to the abandonment of the old form is a time-consuming business; while it is only after the painful experience that we can compare the new form with it and perhaps learn whatever lesson experience has to teach. The waiting, the long delay, and the feeling that time is passing slowly are therefore usually set down to the influence of this planet.

The Ego in the making, rising up out of the ocean of the unconscious, is exposed to make psychic dangers. Its resistance is still small and it takes little to make it lapse into the unmanageable behaviour prompted by the primitive urges. The first conscious experience of oneself as a separate unit is accompanied by feelings of unease. Loneliness, feelings of personal isolation, forelornness and inadequacy are also characteristics of a strong Saturn influence. Protective mechanisms, defence mechanisms and prohibitive regulations result from it. The process of giving form to the Ego within the psyche is outwardly shown by the strong urge to take part in the structuring of external matters.

A constructively employed Saturn factor in the human psyche can give self-control, earnestness, proficiency, accuracy, diligence, perseverance, sense of duty and tenacity, in addition to a methodical and analytical attitude to life. From the fear symbolized by Saturn there flow, on the other hand, characteristics such as unreliability, suspicion, pessimism, fatalism, pettiness, scepticism, heartlessness and obstinate unyieldingness, in addition to a cold, inaccessible and indeed self-conscious attitude.

Wrestling with oneself is central to the Saturn influence in the psyche, and this is one reason why saturnine people are so much involved with themselves. Their inflexible frame of mind, codes of behaviour and other forms are the consequence of the uncertainty felt by the individual who has begun to experience himself consciously. The old astrological tenet that Saturn's actions stem from fear has a new light thrown on it here.

In esoteric astrology Saturn is known as 'the Dweller on the Threshold'. In psychological terms, this means that it is not until man has formed a conscious Ego out of the Ego-complex, through the above-mentioned learning process, that he becomes a real individual. The Saturn process is the sternest test on the path towards Ego-formation.

Another name for Saturn, 'Lord of Karma', clearly refers to the fact that the person himself accepts the responsibility for his own actions and can no longer put the course of events down to the workings of fate. And so, by gaining and comparing experiences, man gains, as already said, an insight into the laws governing cause and effect, enabling him to shape his own destiny.

Once man has pursued the development in himself up to and including the Saturn stage, he can take his place as a full-fledged member of society and as a respected individual. He has then learnt how to function as reliably as possible. Only after this does he enter the stage in which he can delve deeper into the laws of life, and outgrow his intense self-involvement while developing still further in the appreciation of less personal values. As the Mahayana Buddhists would say, the stage of the 'man of normal understanding' is reached at the end of this development under Saturn. The trans-Saturnian planets, comparatively recently discovered, afford an opportunity for further development to the psychological stage of Selfhood or, in Buddhist terms, to the phase of the 'man of superior understanding'.

The Trans-Saturnian Planets
In the development of the human psyche, the phases up to and including that of the formation of a conscious Ego are purely personal in character. The factors symbolized by the sun, moon and planets up to and including Saturn, are in good agreement with these phases. A completely new dimension is

added to the psyche by the trans-Saturnian planets, Uranus, Neptune and Pluto. Since these factors are essentially impersonal, they are often beyond the understanding of the personal part of the psyche. These impersonal factors (which are rooted much deeper in the collective unconscious) do, it is true, acquire a personal colouring when expressed, because they have made themselves evident in human actions. For this reason, it is extremely hard to give a good idea of the impersonal element in describing the methods of expression and reaction patterns symbolized by the trans-Saturnian planets.

Uranus

As will have been gathered from what has just been said, the planets up to and including Jupiter represent direct instinctive drives in man, out of which emerges the Ego-complex, a process symbolized by Saturn. According to Jeff Mayo, however much a man may think that he himself decides just how he will react in a given situation, his reactions are largely conditioned and determined by inherited patterns of instinctive emotional and mental behaviour. He goes on to say, '... but the more evolved the human consciousness becomes, the greater will be his power and intelligence to express himself freely.' The development of consciousness by which the Ego-complex can develop into a strong Ego, is the first step on the way towards transforming the primitive urges. Their further transformation is symbolized in astrology by the planets Uranus, Neptune and Pluto and we can consider these planets as refinements of the existing patterns already mentioned. In the course of human development these refined psychic factors have come to possess behaviour and reaction patterns of their own, which mark them out as distinct dispositions. Nevertheless, they have obviously sprung from primitive human instincts and drives. Just as the need for food to sustain the body can develop into ambition to sustain the Ego-image which, to all appearance, has little to do with food, so the contents of the trans-Saturnian planets are still bound up with the primitive drives of man, even though the mode of expression of these contents seem to stand in isolation. The astrological concept that the planets beyond Saturn are 'higher octaves' of the planets Mercury, Venus and Mars, is corroborated by the modern psychological notion of the transformation of the instinctive drives.

As soon as an Ego proper has been formed, neutral, connected and analytical thought overflows into independent and intuitive thinking and conceiving. Mercurial thought, which is so much concerned with parts and particulars, finds a need, when it has been transformed to Uranian thought, to break through the old limits and frameworks to new dimensions beyond the phenomenal world. Originality, uniqueness and independence in character and thought are typical of the psychic factors symbolized by the planet Uranus. The traditions of the culture to which the individual belongs can do nothing to restrain the independence of his thought: he sees himself as an Ego with its own significance and its own unique approach to life. In a fairly mature personality this Uranus factor can prove liberating; flashes of intuition and genius and an appetite for experimentation can increase individual creativity and even lead to the creation of new forms of living. On the other hand, this factor can become a spur to over-compensation of the destructive kind and there is no reasoning with the individual as he plays the part of rebel or anarchist in order to emphasize or demonstrate his own uniqueness. In this case, the traditional structure of society is categorically rejected, in spite of the danger of 'throwing the baby out with the bathwater'. In a better balanced person, the same psychic factor comes out in a willingness to allow others to live life in the way that pleases them, regardless of how much or little their ideas agree with his own unique outlook.

Uranus stands for the factor in man which, for the sake of self-determination, is all too ready to break up the old patterns, kept in existence by the Saturn function, in order to replace them by patterns and forms which will give the psyche more room for development. Scope for unrestricted and unconditional self-expression is a prerequisite for those with a strong Uranus function, and it can give rise to eccentric behaviour in either a constructive or a destructive sense, when combined with the urge to break through forms. If the circumstances in which the individual finds himself are unduly restricted by rules and regulations, then this function, which is present in us all, can suffer from severe repression, and this can lead to explosive, startling and freakish situations. Hyper-eccentricity, perversity, violent revolution etc. are forms in which this suppressed Uranus factor of the human psyche can then seek an outlet.

The form-destroying character of this Uranus factor means, first of all, the demolition of whatever is experienced as limiting and restrictive in the world outside. Old structures are knocked down to make way for something better and finer. However, in practice it would appear that quite often mankind remains true to what has been demolished and tries to recover what has been lost. From this point of view, Uranus and its demands are destructive; but the person who, in such circumstances, concentrates on seizing the chance to make a new and better start, sees the Uranus factor as a means of release from old ties and obligations.

In the second place, the form-destroying function operates on the man himself and can bring about a metamorphosis in the Ego-structure which has been built up. Understanding and tolerance can grow out of the initial Ego-involvement and rigidity (for which the Saturn phase is responsible), as we have said before. Also there is an increased readiness to recognize the rights of others to hold opinions different from one's own. That is why the communal idea has such an obvious Uranian character thanks to, and in spite of, the Uranian feeling of being a unique individual.

Individuals can find their bearings in a freer and more objective manner and enter more easily into relationships with others when, in the process of breaking down the barriers of their own Ego-structures, they become convinced that everyone's personality is as unique as theirs and that everyone has a relative point of view. With this in mind, they can refrain from interfering with other people's opinions. The danger is, that this manner of relating to others will seem too cold and impersonal. The first possibilities in this direction begin to unfold as adolescence approaches, when the individual is already in a position to experience the law of cause and effect to some extent. M.E. Harding writes:

In the approach to adolescence, the Ego-formation impulse splits into two streams. The first continues in the direction of increasing the strength and prestige of the individual; usually this shows itself most strongly in the urge to dominate others. The sense of being someone is clearly associated with a hankering after power. The second stream now comes into the picture. This moves in the direction of the weakening of the personal Ego for the benefit of the group.

In this planet, too, the constructive properties can change into destructive ones when the individual uses his energy improperly. In the trans-Uranian planets, the destructive action takes a much more serious form than in the so-called classical planets. This has little to do with whether or not they are more 'powerful'; more to the point, it is a confirmation of the old adage that everything has two sides and that the more 'positive' something becomes, the more 'negative' becomes its counterpart. This is reflected in the sayings, 'the greater the intellect, the worse the man', and, 'the higher up, the greater fall'. In this sense the transforming possibilities are greater in the trans-Saturnian planets, and man can reach an awareness that there is more to life than that which simply relates to the Ego.

But the roots of the factors represented by these planets have pushed down deeper into the collective unconscious of man, so that the unconscious activity (with all its associated dangers) can be stronger. On the assumption that human evolution has further to go, many of the contents of these trans-Saturnian planets will naturally still be expressed in an unconscious manner (and often incomprehensibly and even destructively) in familiar and protective situations. Uranus is then the unconscious tendency to chop and change for the sake of it, without really knowing why and without being able to put anything new in place of the old. The other side of the coin is that Uranus can give the intuitive realization that there is more to the world than the phenomena accessible to the sense organs, and the conventional limits are often transcended by a concern with more mystical and occult matters, which have a closer connection with the collective unconscious than has, for example, traditional science.

Owing to the strong link with the unconscious, the mode of expression of the Uranus factor can be sudden and startling – especially as the destruction of forms is so radical. In many instances, the conscious is still not in tune with the less reasonable and therefore unpredictable symbolic contents of the collective unconscious, so that in these instances hints of such contents in the individual's psyche often pass unrecognized. Shock, as an expression of the psychic content of Uranus, can draw the conscious of the individual closer to his own unconscious behaviour and means of expression. It is then possible to have a better interaction between both parts of the psyche and a more complete integration.

Neptune

No better introduction to the astrological meaning of Neptune could be found than this description by the psychologist M.E. Harding.

> And so, at the end of adolescence we usually see a widening and deepening of interests. In the final teenage years and at the start of the twenties, young men and women show a certain amount of attraction to non-personal values. This may express itself in a desire to reform society, in the urge to devote themselves to one or other altruistic project of service to humanity, such as social work or scientific research; it can also emerge in the form of the quest for an ideal romantic love, of a liking for poetry or of absorption in religious experiences. It is as if the Ego, at the very peak of physical growth, is on the point of being replaced by an impersonal principle. However, it is not long before the young person is recalled to reality by the demands of adulthood, with a living to make and a family to support. Circumstances compel a resumption of the struggle to develop the Ego still further and to learn to control it. Usually, the impulse to give up the goals pursued by the Ego for ultra-personal values does not return until the prime of life is over and, as old age approaches, the individual prepares for death.

The Neptune factor signifies a refining of existing psychic contents. In particular, the emotional aspects of experience and the range of experience undergo a change. It is this factor in man that softens and works to improve the hard facts of everyday reality. Thus the world in which he lives seems to form part of a great human ideal which is much more impersonal and much more general in character than that associated with the Jupiter factor in the psyche. Universal love, understanding, warmth and human dedication are typical of Neptune and so the planet has come to be treated as a higher octave of Venus. It is the source in man from which the gifted artist and the devoted religious or secular leader draw their inspiration. These idealizing feelings and this empathy of Neptune can reveal themselves in a number of different ways. Here, too, the contents of what is felt are closely bound up with the collective unconscious, but, just as in the Uranus factor, they can afford an individual greater insight and understanding as they take shape within him. The rich quality of the imagination, the great sensitivity and the strong receptivity of Neptune can prove to be of inestimable value for further development but can also pose a threat to the sense of reality in everyday life. With its power of imagination and capacity for entertaining intense supra-personal feelings, it offers an ideal opportunity for escaping from mundane life into a world of daydreams, into unreal pseudo-religious ideals or fanaticism, into hallucinations (whether or not caused by drug-taking) or into totally submissive self-denial. In a more extreme form, this factor can bring about obsessive, incomprehensible and inexplicable fears and phobias, as well as instability, escapism, a clouded understanding, deception of self and others, and hysteria.

This is a factor in the human psyche which shows to advantage only when the 'test' of Saturn has been passed, that is to say when the formation of the Ego in the process symbolized by Saturn has led to a settled form. The transcending of the old, rigid form to give room for the growth of the individuality and maturity of the personality in a fresh form is therefore what we can term the function of Uranus. After this mastery has been won over form, there follows the stage of Neptune, in which the conscious form is subordinated and the amalgamation with collective, unconscious factors means that we can talk of a certain formlessness. The Ego, as the centre of consciousness, is no longer experienced as the centre of the psyche; it is now integrated within the psyche as a part of the Self. It can take part in natural interchange with the unconscious, the beginning and end point of life. By making contact with the primitive source in this way the individual can experience oneness with life which also comes under Neptune. Taking all this into account, the destructive potential of Neptune is clear. If the still forming, weak Ego exposes itself to the powerful energies of the unconscious, it lays itself open to identification with the unconscious. Under the influence of the unrealistic ideals which the individual identifies himself, he falls into impersonal behaviour in which the developing Ego-complex sinks back again into the ocean of the collective unconscious. The constructive side of Neptune comes to the fore when the form sacrificed to the impersonal and idealistic imagination so characteristic of this planet, is refashioned into a more perfect and more flexible whole in which feeling and thought are better adjusted to one another.

The urge to idealize and the hankering after perfection inherent in the Neptune factor tends to make us look at things 'through rose-coloured spectacles' or, in other words, to experience objective reality subjectively and to indulge in pleasant day-dreams. The outcome, however, may be chaotic, bringing muddle and disorganization. Impostures and frauds are closely associated with this feature, although the deceit is not always practised deliberately. It is highly likely that a distortion of facts occurs even at the moment of observation, making it impossible to report them correctly.

Thus Neptune's facility for softening our impressions can be as much bemusing and confusing as it is helpful, even if it does extend the range of the mind and enable it to penetrate to the world of universal spiritual values in trances and visions.

Owing to the considerable extent to which the feelings play a part in this psychic factor, the fundamental meaning of the planet is difficult to put into words. Words belong to our conscious personality, while the emotional life is much more close to the unconscious area of the psyche. Refinement of the emotions puts man in a position to gain experience transcending all forms and structures and his emotional responses can supply him with the inspiration to elevate himself to a higher state of perfection and fulfilment. Neptune, then, is the symbol of a love of humanity, subtlety, romanticism, tenderness, sensitivity and mysticism.

But this emotional life which is so incomprehensible to the intellect can also make the person susceptible to the attractions of artificially idealized fantasy worlds, and the Neptune factor can show itself in the form of a need for glamour and false glitter or of ecstatic and unconventional sensory experiences. For the very reason that this factor is emotional and vague, the processes taking place in the psyche are not perceived directly and, by the time their destructive nature has become apparent, it is too late to do anything about it. On the other hand, the factor can unconsciously lead him to a deeper appreciation of his world and, without knowing it, he can benefit from his empathy with others and his sensitivity to their feelings.

If an individual consciously clings to his picture of himself, his contact with his unconscious will be more uneasy than if he learnt to view himself more relatively through his trans-Saturnian side. The pure action of Neptune is hampered and the factors concerned often emerge twisted and deformed; the Ego-image is lacking in harmony and there may be an addiction to drugs, drink and dreams, possibly accompanied by dishonesty.

The deeper rooted the contents of the human psyche in the collective unconscious, the greater is the possibility of transformation such as is symbolized by the trans-Saturnian planets. The contents are more comprehensive and promising on the one hand and more difficult to understand on the other, so that the individual can pose a threat to himself and in spite of the possibilities in the direction of transcendence his personality can disintegrate.

Pluto

In the early days of human life, just as in the life of a baby, life was controlled by the forces of instinct. But there comes a time when another force arises which puts a stop to the free play of instinctive wishes and desires. To a certain extent, this force is active in us all, even in the most primitive human. We call it the will. The energy which maintains it is withdrawn from the instincts and is used by the Ego which came into existence as soon as the instincts were restrained.

At the moment the Ego-complex succeeds in abstracting energy from the instincts, there is a great chance the still uncertain Ego-image will fall into the power of these energies and identify itself with them; beginning to develop a power complex. At the same time as the Ego is formed out of the sea of the unconscious a new problem arises, therefore: the wish to have a power-base. Since this hankering after power is at the expense of the instincts, it cannot be regarded as one of the instincts, even though it displays the same compulsive character in many respects. What is more, this power-complex should not be identified with the Ego-complex, which is preliminary to the fully formed Ego-image. It is a psychic expression which must be recognized for what it is; a separate complex, however close its connection with the formation of the Ego. This power-complex, which can lead a man to complete ruin or to fabulous achievements, is symbolized in astrology by the last planet – Pluto.

The function of the Pluto factor in the human psyche is extremely critical; it is, to quote Jeff Mayo, '... a natural outlet for bringing to the surface those repressed and lost factors out of the personal unconscious.' The force with which these factors seek an outlet becomes greater the more forcibly and decisively a person represses his complex and what he feels are the unacceptable sides of his nature. This psychic content is then responsible for powerful emotional, hysterical and almost volcanic outbursts, in which, at one blow, problems, difficulties, tensions, emotional disturbances etc. rise up and thrust themselves into consciousness. After such outbursts, it is hardly possible to return to the old state of affairs as if nothing had happened. The Pluto factor forces the individual, so to speak, to the liquidation or transformation of the emergent contents by assimilation or integration.

It is this Pluto factor that constitutes the biggest force in the human unconscious for keeping the conscious mind on the strait and narrow path, if need be by giving the inflated Ego a sudden prick. 'Inflated' means here an exaggeration of the conscious personality because suprapersonal factors are caught up in the Ego. The resistance offered to conscious recognition of one's own repressed problems and complexes – often strengthened because the individual tries to rationalize his behaviour, and thereby clings to it all the longer – gives rise to neurotic tendencies; another way in which the Pluto factor can find expression. When the things mentioned cannot be brought out into the open, the person's unconscious seeks an outlet in various symptoms which gradually become more pronounced and should serve as warning signals to the conscious mind. But the danger is that the individual will become increasingly governed by these repressed factors in his unconscious until the point is reached where the latter come completely to control his behaviour and wishes. Then, in spite of the fact that it has emerged from the unconscious and may already have undergone considerable development, the Ego starts to disintegrate again and is occupied by factors belonging to the unconscious, so that the individual concerned is no longer 'personal' but represents a collective archetype. This is one of the greatest dangers continually threatening the human psyche and a severe crisis and/or a great psychic shock is required to free the individual from his incarceration in collective, impersonal states of mind.

A phenomenon closely connected with the above and also belonging to Plutonic conditions, is what Carl Jung calls the 'mana personality'. This is a positive inflation of the Ego, in which the Ego feels powerful, influential and dominant, must always be in the right and sees itself as the lord and master. Anyone who is affected like that, unconsciously identifies himself with a great historical figure such as Christ for example, or Napoleon, seeing himself more and more as the leader of a group of people or even of the whole of mankind. In this he can meet with considerable success, so long as he is able to find followers or at least encounters little opposition from outside. However, he remains totally undeveloped as a person; his Ego is at the mercy of the energy he has borrowed and has itself been assimilated to unconscious instinctive drives. And so, the power-complex can be formed and by a failing to recognize the process in good time, by ignoring the symptoms or by deliberately running away from an untenable situation, the Ego starts to identify more and more strongly with energy purloined from the unconscious, no longer realizing that it has very little say in what the individual says and does. Everything is arranged by the growing power-complex and, at a certain moment, the point is reached when it is no longer possible to deal with the individual on a give-and-take basis. Criticism serves only to strengthen such an individual in the idea that he is some sort of misunderstood martyr. Everything he encounters in the way of criticism is interpreted solely in terms of this obsession which, at its most grave, can lead to insanity – the total disintegration of the individuality.

Carl Jung calls the image with which a person identifies

himself in the course of developing a mana personality, the 'magician'. Identification is consistently made with powers that are occult and magical or, 'superhuman'. Jung goes on to say:

> In women, the figure of the magician takes on a no less dangerous equivalent guise, ie that of a maternal figure, the All Mother, who will be merciful to all, who understands everything and forgives everything, who has always wanted the best for others, who lives for them and never consults her own wishes. She has also discovered the Great Love just as her male counterpart has found the Only Truth to promulgate. And just as the Only Truth is never appreciated at its true value, so the Great Love is never understood. Neither finds the other wholly bearable.

The identification of oneself with either the archetypal image of the Great Father or that of the Great Mother, as the case may be, reveals that unconscious rein has been given to the lust for power, in which the psychic content of Pluto is involved. Especially at a time like the present, in which procedures and methods for heightening awareness have almost become a cult, an individual is very likely to fall victim to the unconscious forces he has unleashed and which he is, as yet, unable to cope with.

Man's Pluto component is forcing him, now more than ever before, to balance on a knife-edge. The more man goes on from the Ego stage to the stage of Self, the more this component will sharpen that knife-edge, in the extremely critical process brought about by Pluto. While recognizing that this planet has a clearly destructive aspect, we do have to bear in mind that at the present stage of human development, the Pluto factor is a particularly refined psychic instrument and perhaps too advanced to be kept under control. The transforming function is expressed in the ability (or perhaps it would be nearer the mark, where the Saturnian phase is concerned, to say, 'is expressed in the unconscious urge') to get inside the psychic mechanism and to penetrate to the repressed contents in the personal unconscious. The personal unconscious is the borderland between the conscious mind and the collective unconscious and should form a layer permitting a living interaction between the two instead of dividing the contents of consciousness and of the collective unconscious and making polarization possible. In this function we see Pluto at work as a remover of rubbish and obstructions so that the development of the individual and of the race can proceed on its way. But as long as this force is not controlled by our conscious mind, we are exposed to the danger of becoming trapped when we try to delve into the unconscious. Hence each of us runs the risk of returning to the status of an impersonal, collective person and being scarcely more than something governed by a power-complex in the unconscious.

The collective activity ascribed in astrology to Pluto, can be understood better if we bear in mind that the Pluto factor is for the most part unconscious and has only very recently begun to play a part in human development. Many feelings, emotions and the like affect an individual at the unconscious level of his mind and so it is possible to 'play on' men and masses. In the period between the two World Wars (Pluto was discovered in 1930) both the collective and the individual power complex manifested itself to its full extent. It speaks for itself that to stir up the masses, there must be something to draw on. The collective cruelty which can be brought into the open by this factor is (notwithstanding its frightfulness) a scaling up of the Pluto function within the psyche of the individual. When expressing itself in a Plutonian manner, the crowd (in a lynching party for example) tried to rid itself of the 'evil' in its ranks. At a still more abstract and more incomprehensible level this collective factor manifests in wholesale disasters. However, other mysterious elements (such as the Mafia and multinational companies) are also ruled by Pluto.

These little understood forces can lead an individual to self-destruction in which others are involved as a sort of collective fate. But this is only one side of Pluto. As far as we know, Pluto is the outermost planet of our solar system and in our inner universe, too, the things represented by Pluto reach furthest. The destruction typical of the plutonic, can also indicate that in us which spoils our lives and makes us cling to the Ego, giving it the opportunity to regard itself as the uncrowned king of the consciousness and of the whole psyche, since all it perceives is the world above the threshold of consciousness. Nevertheless, Pluto, who in mythology is the god of the underworld, can undermine the upper world if we ignore his kingdom and block all access to it. It is significant that the plutonic power-complex emerges from the collective unconscious simultaneously with the Ego. Pluto is certainly a critical factor in the psyche. He stands for the compelling impulse towards the integration of all parts of the psyche, and that means constant renewal and continuous adaptation to the needs of individual and collective evolution. In this sense, Pluto is not the metamorphosis itself but the power that keeps on impelling us in the direction of renewal, of death and rebirth.

Pluto is the last planet to be discovered and, in a way, this symbolizes the difficulty we have in experiencing what it brings and the even greater difficulty in handling it. Just as Saturn, the Dweller on the Threshold, in the past used to signify 'transition', so Pluto, at the extreme edge of our solar system now marks the staging-post for the transition from the Ego to the Self.

8

Growth and Development

A Qabalistic Legend
In his *Analytical Psychology*, Dr Gerhard Adler refers to an old Qabalistic legend on the making of man, a legend which recounts that at the moment of procreation, God calls the germ of the future being before Him to decide the terms of existence of the new soul: whether it will be male or female, rich or poor, wise or foolish and so on. Only one decision is left open, whether the person will be righteous or an evil-doer; for 'Everything lies in the hands of God, except the fear of God.' The legend goes on to describe how the soul pleads not to be sent from that world to this. But God answers, 'The world to which I am now sending you is better than the world in which you were and, when I created you, I destined you for this earthly lot.' On speaking these words, God entrusts the soul to the angel in charge of all souls in the other world. The angel reveals to her all the secrets of the other world and conducts her through Heaven and Hell. When she is born in this world, however, the angel extinguishes the Light of Knowledge, and the soul is inserted into an earthly sheath without the Great Secret which she will have to win back.

Adler interprets the first part of this legend as follows:

... each of us is given a certain lot in life; for each is a path appointed – but whether or not a man will fulfil his destiny instead of going his own way is in his own hands. The fear of God, the recognition of the divine destiny of man ... is different for each one of us. For each one the goal is fixed, but the way to it, its attainment, is a matter for the individual. Truly, this is a deep answer to the age-old problem of free will.

In the conceptual framework of Jung's psychology, the other world of which the legend speaks can be seen as the collective unconscious of man, within which lie the primitive experiences of humanity. It is accessible to all, because it forms part of each individual psyche and yet it lies beyond the reach of conscious reason in a state of dormancy. It contains the matrices of all human knowledge and activities. The mythical world of the young child and the symbolic language of dreams are where it shows itself. At the moment an individual enters the world, the Ego-complex starts to develop; the process of growing self-awareness, in which the mental and logical side of the human psyche become clearly defined at the expense of the more primitive collective unconscious in which the instinctive drives are stored. As already seen when the contents of the planets were discussed, there lies concealed in this duality of conscious *versus* unconscious, the possibility of regaining what the legend calls the Great Secret (Great Knowledge), but this time consciously.

The agreement between the Qabalah, psychology and astrology on this essential point is quite striking. From an astrological point of view, man is even less of a blank sheet at birth than the Qabalistic legend represents him to be; indeed, in babies of a few days old certain features present in their horoscopes are already quite apparent. The child is born with a specific psychic structure and has a unique set of characteristics which is mirrored in the individual constellation of the natal horoscope. The said horoscope contains his possibilities, limitations and difficulties from birth onwards: the problem he will encounter, the things that give him sorrow or joy, the lessons he must learn and the gifts which will bear fruit. In short, everything is present in potential form but it is the individual himself who will decide whether or not the possibilities will be realized.

The development undergone by this individual can be inferred from the various kinds of progressions and transits that occur in the successive stages of his life. They are patterns of internal and external change, offering changes of development and scope for gaining experience in different areas. By living we can become aware of many realities and facets of life. For example, over a period of twenty-four hours, we observe that it is light during the day and dark at night. Noticing the difference, we are aware of a fact of nature that can have an influence on what we do. Essential activities in the open air will be done when it is still light, bearing in mind the verified fact that darkness will return. Although this is a simple example, the principle that experience is gained by noting differences is very important, and a direct consequence of this line of reasoning is that we are dependant on time. Events happen in the course of time which can be put in relationship with one another, referred to one another and compared by one another. Experience arises out of this temporal process and as we grow older there is an increasing chance that mature wisdom will be the result.

Time and Cycles

The cycle is a special mode in which events can take place in time. We know many astronomical cycles, a number of which are very important in astrology. Dane Rudhyar's comment is relevant here when he says, '... astrology may be defined as a technique for studying life cycles. Its main objective is to determine the existence of regular patterns in the succession of events, patterns deciding internal experiences and events. Once found, these patterns can be used to control or interpret experiences and events.

Thus the sun takes an annual course through the individual horoscope. The points in the horoscope with which it makes contact in the process will be those psychic factors which are or can be of current interest over the short term. In this way one can examine all the transits of all the planets and of the sun and moon. Nevertheless, it is not every planet that makes a complete circuit in a single lifetime. Considering that Uranus can make its first return to the place it occupied in the horoscope at birth if the native lives to the age of eighty-four, it will be realized that death will have overtaken him before the planets Neptune and Pluto make a similar return. Yet although we can talk of the cycle of Uranus in an astronomical sense, its cycle has a 'non-cyclic' once-only meaning from an astrological point of view. Its single trip round the horoscope makes it impossible for there to be a repetition of a transit over the same point within a human lifetime. Thus the assimilation of and the building on the experiences under the previous transit, so essential to astrological cycles in the natal horoscope, are excluded. A cycle is, by definition, an interval of time within which there takes place a characteristic and, especially, a repeated event or series of events.

It is only in time that man can gain experience and undergo and assimilate events, but human life is spent within a given limited period. For our purposes, the duration of human life is what matters for finding the most significant planetary cycles, not the fact that from an astronomical point of view *all* planets make regular cyclic movements.

In itself, 'life' is an abstract concept, with which we can come to terms only when it reveals itself in the material world that is accessible to the senses; in other words when it takes a form. Life can express itself in an endless variety of forms both in animals and plants and one of these many forms is man. Astrology recognizes the idea of 'form' under two planets. Fixed form is determined by Saturn and fluid form by the moon, which may in fact be regarded as the living content within fixed form. It is a remarkable fact that these heavenly bodies having a relationship with form both go round the horoscope three times during a human lifetime, assuming the latter to last eight-four years. Saturn does this by actual transit with a time of revolution of 29.5 years; the moon takes 28 years by secondary progression. The duration of both cycles is therefore near enough alike.

This noteworthy coincidence between the quickest (the moon) and the slowest heavenly body (Saturn), if we confine ourselves to the planets known to classical astrology (those we have dubbed the 'personal' ones), becomes even more important in the light of the fact that both planets (or psychic factors) have to do with the form and formation or learning process of life: the moon as an assimilating and reproductive faculty and Saturn as a structuring force and as the 'process of learning through pain', as Liz Greene puts it. In the development of the individual, these cycles are therefore the background to the formation of the Ego and the building up of a genuine individuality or, as so imaginatively expressed in the old Qabalistic legend of the making of man, to winning the Great Secret in following the road to self-determination.

The Cycles of the Moon and Saturn and the Father and Mother Complexes

Taken as psychic factors, the moon and Saturn are very closely associated with the so-called 'father' and 'mother complexes', in which the word 'complex' need not necessarily have a negative connotation. The psychologists Carl Jung and Gerhard Adler both point to the fact that a complex can also have a positive effect, namely when acting as a lens to focus the psychic energy in a certain direction (usually too intensely however), and that then it can result in unusual performance. It is premised in this case that the mind is able to 'handle' the complex.

June Singer probably gave as good a definition as any when she explained that they are certain constellations of psychic elements (ideas, opinions, convictions etc.) which are so to speak gathered around emotionally sensitive areas. Such a complex consists of two parts: a nucleus serving as a kind of magnet and attracting the second component, the swarm of associations which can settle round the nucleus. The nucleus itself also comprises two parts. One part is determined by experience and is therefore bound up with the environment. The other part is determined by the innate constitution or disposition of the individual in question. When an individual, with the character peculiar to himself, finds it impossible to make a crucial decision himself, he suffers a psychic trauma which may start or contribute to a complex. This can exercise a disturbing effect on the aims, the will and the output of the conscious mind. Carl Jung adds that these complexes can disturb the workings of memory and cause the stream of associations to stagnate. Complexes come and go in their own sweet way and also have an unconscious influence on words and deeds. (Sigmund Freud gratefully used this contribution of Jung's to psychotherapy, and that is why slips of the tongue arising from complexes in the unconscious are still invariably called 'Freudian slips'.)

An important element in any complex is its emotional loading. Generally speaking, the complex forms in the field of consciousness the picture of a disturbed mental situation which is strongly coloured emotionally and seems to be inconsistent with the ordinary conscious attitude or state of mind. More often than not, this leads to a moral conflict. The deepest cause of the conflict is apparently the impossibility of accepting one's own character traits as a whole.

Nobody is entirely free of complexes, so complexes have little to do with inferiority; on the contrary, these centres of functional disturbance, though they may be a hindrance and a source of conflict in the psyche, do represent a potential stimulus to the creation of new opportunities and the winning of success. 'In this sense, therefore, complexes are simple centres and nodes in the psychic life, which it would be better for man not to miss nor indeed have lacking, since otherwise the psychic activity would come to a standstill'. So says Carl Jung and adds, '... in every instance they point to what is incomplete in the individual and thus to the real weak spot in every sense of the word.'

As already explained, the nucleus of a complex consists of an innate part and a part formed by the experiences of the individual. The innate part, the part that forms the pattern and is as it were the matrix of the complex can be traced back to what Jung calls an 'archetype': the immaterial root idea already present before psychic contents and images crystallize out (see Chapter 1). Thus pre-images already seem to lie dormant in the psyche, in the layer Jung calls the collective unconscious. They wait there to be 'brought to life' in a personal way and to play a part in the development of the person concerned. Wholly based on the psyche is the archetype of the Self, the inner unity, the life force and life source. Some have termed it the 'god in us'. This Self is a quantity manifesting itself in the duality of existence, as comes out so clearly in the quotation from the Tao Teh King at the head of Chapter 2. Even the duality of male and female lies hidden as an archetype in the human collective unconscious and assumes living shape as the father and mother images, images which also have a connection with our internal image of our partner – the anima in the case of the man and the animus in the case of the woman. (See Chapter 6).

When a man enters the world, he brings with him an inborn picture of what a father and mother is, based on the latent images of the male and female principles in the collective unconscious shared by all men. He projects these latent images on the people he regards and accepts as parents (who need not necessarily be his parents in the biological sense. The possession of *de facto* parents is what is decisive for the child's psyche and development, regardless of any blood relationship). Therefore, the father and mother idea is present in us as an 'ideal image' even before we are able to recognize our parents as such. Each ideal and desire in the psyche seeks incarnation and, for the child, the ideal mother and father image are embodied in his parents. However, when the individual grows older and the process begins by which he disengages himself from his parents and from the parental environment, new bearers of the father and mother archetypes must be sought by a process which takes place wholly in the unconscious. It is necessary for a person to go through this process in order to achieve a balanced development and individuation. The moon and Saturn as the symbols of certain psychic factors play a vital rôle here.

Together, the moon and Saturn represent the function of the child's parents. Ideally, the child learns adjustment to circumstances from its mother (the moon), and a sense of order and restraint from its father (Saturn), of whom it stands in awe. A powerful Saturn in the horoscope can symbolize a powerful father and a strong moon a forceful mother. There is no hard-and-fast rule that the father or mother will, in fact, be dominant in this way; more usually, the child will experience them as such. Individual experiences during the lifetime merely serve to fill the mould already supplied in the unconscious.

When one of the said heavenly bodies in the horoscope of the native is much stronger than the other, by placement in sign and house and by aspect, it is very likely that a complex will be formed in the person's psyche in keeping with the nature of the planet concerned. Once again, it must be emphasized that such a complex need not have a negative effect. It will however play a decisive part in the process of becoming independent from the parents; a radical step in life that can be taken in many different ways. Some folk, for instance, always remain dependent on their parents, others gradually learn to stand on their own two feet, and yet others strike out on their own at a very early age. An inner process that goes hand in hand with becoming independent from the actual parents – and one overlooked by astrologers pretty often – is the so-called transcendence of the father and mother image.

A weak moon in the horoscope can mean that, when he is young, the mother has not succeeded in giving the child a sufficient sense of security and safety so that, later in life, he will go looking (usually unconsciously) for the safety and protection it has missed. When someone affected like this reaches the point where the male and female archetypes become detached from his real father and mother and he starts to make his own way in the world (with regard to his inner life, anyway, even if he does not go into lodgings), then, although the father and mother archetypes have transcended their original containers, the inadequacy of that first mother-contact, in the example cited, can lead him to look for safety and protection in more abstract forms. Collective entities such as the church, the native land, a political party and even a certain type of 'faith' in astrology, frequently figure in the need for a transcendent mother image. When astrology is regarded as a divine law, rigid and unalterable, we should look for the influence of Saturn and of a transcendent father image.

Dane Rudhyar has interested himself in analyzing the use of astrology in regard to these father and mother complexes and he raises a number of useful points on the matter. Taking our cue from him, we can find the following ways in which astrology is treated when it is directly linked with a father or mother complex. Naturally, one can also envisage many intermediate forms.

i) As a trascendental mother image, astrology lays the main emphasis on fate. This occurs when there is a weak Saturn function in the horoscope. Fate is inescapable and submission to it represents in fact an undeveloped sense of individuality and form. Planets are often regarded as entities which actually exercise a good or bad influence and the person concerned sees himself as dependant on the all-governing 'stars', which is very much the same as looking for the 'Great Mother', a phenomenon extensively researched by Erich Neumann. (See Erich Neumann: *The Great Mother*. Details in *Bibliography*.) The individual sense of responsibility is minimal here and is not developed further.

ii) When the Saturn function is over-developed, theoretical and technical analyses and reasoning predominate and, as Dane Rudhyar says, the astrologer can '... lose himself in theories and formulae regarding the Self and the universe and regarding cycles and abstract patterns ... so that he fails to see the practical solution necessary for a successful confrontation with immediate personal needs. ... He searches for an all-embracing, universal or divine plan designed for a rationally constructed world of pure forms and cosmic qualities, because he perceives within himself a continual flow of irrational life-tides (the moon), disorder or a lack of harmony over which he has no mental control.' As the individual detaches himself inwardly from dependence on his actual father he pursues the father-image further in making himself dependant on an ordered cosmic law in the person of God or a transcendental all-inclusive father figure.

Of course, the practice of astrology need not be an escape route for non-assimilated father and mother factors; the above example is given merely to show how escapism might work. Astrology, provided it is approached in an adult manner, can just as easily be educative and can provide an insight into life-cycles. The individual learns to exercise his privileges and responsibilities within the framework of his own nature, is helped to take fairly balanced decisions and, above all, comes to know himself because he dares to be himself.

We see, then, how the cycles of the moon and Saturn can tell us something about the factors which play a rôle in the processes of development, learning to become an individual and maturing into a ripe old age. The father and mother images in the psyche, enlivened by archetypal factors, are closely involved here and remain with us throughout our lives. It is the cycles of the moon and Saturn which present a person with the possibilities and problems of making something of his father and mother images and of endeavouring to increase his personal awareness. The degree to which the individual genuinely learns to make room for whatever is brought to him on his path through life by the cycles we are discussing, is the degree to which he fulfils the destiny for which he was born, as described in the Qabalistic legend.

The Three Successive Cycles: an Overall View

The three revolutions made by the moon and Saturn through the individual horoscope indicate that the native undergoes as many as three cycles of development. This development, being spiral, can manifest on three different levels. During the first twenty-eight years of our lives we are mainly concerned with what Marc Robertson terms the 'creation of a vehicle for operating in society'. We are strongly under the influence of our parents and of the things they have taught us. In addition, various cultural and social forces have a big influence on the formation of the vehicle and especially on its structure. It is a phase in which many of us experience that we are simply playing a part and that we are no more than what our environment and our immediate circle will allow. We are not our true selves. The moon and Saturn complete their first trip round the horoscope in twenty-eight years and, at the end of this period, the finishing touches have been put to the vehicle in which we hold our own in society – or hope to do so. The second cycle is now ushered in, and particular importance is attached to the formation of an identity and the finding of our own unique manner of self-expression.

The first time Saturn transits its position at birth and the moon returns to its place by secondary direction, Uranus makes its first trine with its own place in the horoscope. This means that we can raise our cultural identity (Saturn) to a higher level in tune with our individualtiy (Uranus). And so the transforming (Uranus) of the structure that has been formed (Saturn) can commence. The second period of twenty-eight years is typified by this transformation and can improve the structure of the individual. The ease or difficulty with which this process takes place may be gathered from the aspects made with other planets, and with their own places in the horoscope, by the transiting planets. The individual development is further supplemented by the perfectly unique, individual progression which gives shape to the succeeding cycles in a personal manner.

The period of life between the ages of twenty-eight and thirty brings a totally unexpected identity crisis for many people. In modern Western society, we assume that a person is grown up at the age of twenty-one; full adulthood, however, does not occur until the age of thirty,* when the moon and Saturn have made one circuit of the horoscope and have touched and aspected each point in it in all possible ways. Thus, in this first development the individual is confronted by all his psychic factors from various 'angles'. Statistics reveal the social consequences of this crisis. Many marriages break up in this period and lots of people suddenly change their spheres of activity or study, etc.

After the second circuit of the moon and Saturn as formative forces has ended, and the age of fifty-six to sixty is reached, we come to the time of life when we have to 'find ourselves' in the setting of what Carl Jung calls the individuation process. This is the commencement of the third period: the unfolding of inner spiritual powers. The lifetime between fifty-six and sixty years of age sees another crisis of identity. This time, however, it is not concerned with the urge to break free from the forces and forms outside the individual (the cultural saturnine powers); it has to do with the individuality in a rather different way. The individuality has to learn to develop (Uranus). It is Neptune now which comes to the fore; Saturn has once more returned to its own place and so has the moon by secondary progression. Uranus too comes into the picture, making its second trine with its own place. Neptune sets a new task in life for the person entering this third cycle: the realization of the fact that, although he has or should have completed an individual task in life, the time has now come for him to let go of his exclusive individualism and to commit himself to that from which he emerged. We are talking about the personal and collective unconscious, or the ability of the person to link up with the primary powers in the cosmos that bestowed life on him. It is obvious that very many people stick at this point and cling to the tried and trusted forms associated with the past (Saturn), which they should have already assimilated. There is also a destructive side to the Neptune factor which can make itself

---

*As an interesting side-light on this view, it may be mentioned that the Old Testament Levites were not called to serve God until they were thirty and that Christ's ministry began at about this age.   *Translator's note.*

felt in this final phase. Instead of finding oneself, feeling at one with everything and enjoying a deep insight into life, one can fall back on vague ideals and memories in a 'second childhood'. Carl Jung emphasizes more than once that elderly people have to abandon the idea that their lives can develop any further inside a social framework but that they should engage in further consolidation. An inexorable inner process goes on which results in a contraction of life. In a young person it is almost a sin and certainly a danger to be overconcerned with himself, but for older folk it is an obligation and, indeed, a necessity to give themselves some serious thought. Jung writes in his *Modern Man in Search of a Soul*:

> After the sun has lavished his light on the world, he withdraws his rays to illuminate himself. But instead of copying him, all too many elderly people choose to go on living as hypochondriacs, as niggling dogmatists, as worshippers of the past or as eternal adolescents, all of which are deplorable substitutes for the enlightenment of the Self, but are the inevitable results of the delusion that, in the second half of life, the principles governing the first half are still applicable.

Taking a bird's-eye view of the process of development in man, we see that in youth there is a big struggle to release the Ego from the unconscious. In adulthood the Ego is increasingly shaped by events and experiences and, in the process of individuation, the first steps are taken along the road to genuine self-knowledge, which in later years can lead to an eventual understanding of life and of the Self. The Self is understood here as that indivisible nucleus in man which aims at uniting the unconscious side of the psyche with its conscious side. In one big effort at development in later life, the psyche endeavours to counterbalance the separation of the Ego out of the unconscious mind which took place in youth, by bringing about a conscious reunion of both parts of the psyche. In other words, it tries to make wisdom flower out of knowledge.

Developmental Tendencies in the Child
As appears from the foregoing, it is possible to distinguish developmental tendencies which are obviously common to

everybody, quite apart from idiosyncrasies of individual character also reflected in the horoscope. Hidden behind the diversity is a universal trend which starts at birth and ends in death and this universal cycle, stripped of all possible personal elements, will now be discussed.

Birth, the moment that decides the structure of the natal horoscope, is the first great life-shock experienced by the child. As yet, there is no conscous awareness and no Ego-feeling. In the first years of childhood, life is determined by a multitude of images and forms which have their origin in the collective unconscious part of the psyche. It is a mythical world, a fairy-tale world, with all the possibilities contained therein – all the enchantment, all the terror and all the dreams. The child lives a day at a time, has no conception of the reality of the present and is consciously aware of very few things. He is still living purely instinctively and his reactions are in response to instinctive drives. In these early years there is as yet no question of a continuous or coherent memory; at best there are small islands of consciousness in the ocean of the unconscious, like tiny lights in the dark expanse of night.

The Ego begins to form itself out of these little islands of consciousness and, right at the start the Ego itself is just one of these islands. That is why the child speaks of itself in the third person as if it were an objective and independent entity. This is seen to occur at the moment when Saturn forms a semi-sextile with its place in the natal horoscope, while the moon also makes a semi-sextile by secondary progression with its radical place. The child then learns his name and manages to find his place in the family. This happens at some time between the ages of two and three. Afterwards, the quantity of things entering consciousness begins to increase rapidly and the child enters a period when contact with others plays a steadily growing rôle in a first essay in social living. Between the third and fourth year he becomes more outgoing and now clearly identifies himself with his own name. The Ego emerges more distinctly from the collective unconscious and the feeling of being a separate someone begins to show itself.

Towards the end of the third year of life, the child really manages to say 'I', at a moment when subjectivity starts to play a part in the child's life. From an astrological point of view, we see that at the point when the Ego of the child breaks free from its collective unconscious, Saturn and the moon both make a semi-square with the radical position; the first attempt at socialization expresses itself with the first square Jupiter makes with itself.

In the years following the moment of saying 'I', development is very flexible. In astrology, the sextile and quintile of the moon and Saturn succeed the semi-square aspect. The child is constantly learning new things every day by experiences and contacts. The memory for facts improves, even though comparatively few things can be fully grasped by the conscious mind at this stage. There are few, if any, internal problems. Everything that represents a problem is part of an experience in the world outside the child himself and, anyway, he has little real interest in that world. The fairy-tale world and 'magical thinking' (the 'participation mystique' as Levi-Brühl called it) still have pride of place. The outer world is experienced as lying on the borders of the inner world.

All is altered, however, in the seventh to eighth year, when the moon and Saturn make their first square with their respective natal positions. The accompanying inner tension produces behaviour which exhibits aggression and an obvious intention to hold one's own. More is expected of the child too. His kindergarten days are over and he is learning how to 'keep in step' and to do more of what is expected of him. The activity of the square expresses itself in behaviour which is no longer unconscious and directed to living in an internal mythical world but is concerned with a much more realistic approach. The child attaches increasing importance to describing things as they are, begins to show interest in the world outside and is eager to learn.

Around the age of nine to ten years, he has become quite sophisticated in expressing himself in this raw, realistic manner. He can stand on his own two feet pretty confidently and, in general, enters a care-free period. The moon and Saturn now move on to make a trine with their radical positions and Jupiter goes from a quintile to a sextile aspect with its own place in the horoscope. These relatively easy aspects can give the growing child a feeling of complacency so that at the age of eleven or twelve he goes to meet the world with boldness. The external world presents him with a challenge now and he begins to have a stronger sense of his own identity. After a while tensions can result from this attitude in respect of self-esteem. Astrologically, this shows up in the sesquiquadrate of the moon and Saturn and, what is very significant, in the semi-square now formed by Uranus with its radical position. The child begins to show more marked individual traits. A process is going on which adds a fresh dimension to the Ego under formation, a process accompanied by new feelings and experiences. Sexuality starts to be aroused, thus introducing a new phase in life. This is the age at which Jupiter has completed its first transit through the horoscope and re-occupied its original position. The moon and Saturn each form a biquintile and new possibilities present themselves in the child's psyche.

All this happens in a period that precedes one of the early crises in life, known to us as puberty. Up to puberty, although he does not realize it, the child is completely dependant on his parents; he identifies himself with them and feels a part of them. We might even say that, although the child is already there in a biological sense, he has to wait until puberty for his psychic birth. Gerhard Adler writes in his *Analytical Psychology*: 'During the years of early childhood it is mainly the parents' archetypes which, as representatives of the collective unconscious, form the antipole of the individual Ego. This also explains why the influence of the parents has such a far-reaching effect on the actual personality.' This unconscious influence of the parents on the child's psyche is made possible by the psychic factors in the child himself, factors which are present from birth. The experiences connected with these parent images or archetypes of father and mother are symbolized by the moon and Saturn, both in the child's experiences in the world outside and in its own psyche. These ought not to be treated as separate and, because the sun and moon still work so unconsciously in these first years of life, the significance of their movements is all the more essential. Their formative action is hardly restrained by the conscious Ego of the child, which is still wholly open to its own inner world and to influences from outside. That is why the instinctive drives are still decisive for the attitude and the reactions.

Until puberty, the child is not really in conflict with himself. He operates as a unity; external limitations do not usually become internal obstacles. It is only at puberty that the situation changes, when the 'psychic birth' takes place. Adler continues:

> The whole of life can be considered as a process of adaptation to factors which have an *a priori* existence. We ourselves are born, but both the archetypes and the internal worlds (the latter being that of the archetypes and of the collective unconscious) consist of pre-existing realities which are always there ... The Ego germ, the veritable X-factor in life ... has to adapt to the inner and outer realities; it must assimilate them and experience them individually. Without this Ego, which experiences and digests the 'inner' and the 'outer', the whole world would simply not exist psychologically.

In these words, Gerhard Adler highlights the first crisis in human life encountered by the individual: experience of the antithesis between the inner world and the outer world in a way that brings the child into conflict with himself.

Puberty and Adolescence

Whereas the years between eight and twelve are relatively simple, studious, vital and docile, those between twelve and seventeen present a quite different picture. There is an introspective, dualistic attitude, mainly brought about by the far-reaching physical changes taking place at this time of life. The organism is thrown off balance for a considerable period to a greater or lesser degree by the changes in internal secretion (the secretions of the endocrine glands) and by sexual maturation. At this time, the differences between boys and girls (not merely the physical ones but more importantly the psychic ones too) become quite obvious. It is a period which could be termed the 'negative phase', there is a departure from the former normal behaviour and, above all, the child distances himself or herself from earlier authorities and friends to an increasing extent. New interests and activities come to the fore and push most of the old interests into the background. Everything points to the termination of one period before a new life-style has been formed.

Puberty usually commences around the time when Saturn and the moon make their first inconjunct (or quincunx) aspects with their own radical places. Apparently insoluble and out-of-the-ordinary tensions build up in the psyche of the developing child. A need is felt to depart from the inculcated codes and standards of behaviour, while at the same time the budding sexuality arouses the emotional life in a manner not previously experienced. This emotional upheaval however, which can become so all-absorbing, the irrational tensions, the accelerated growth of the body that can throw it out of proportion, are but a few of the many things which may make the vulnerable child feel so insecure in this period ...

The uncertainty – viewed astrologically – reaches an all-time low when the moon and Saturn reach their first opposition, as normally happens between fourteen and fifteen years of age. At this time of life the behaviour is often avowedly anti-social, due to overcompensation for the uncertainty over the inner emotional life and the external position in the world. Many children now feel misunderstood and seek refuge in solitary day-dreams, in drugs, in juvenile delinquency, etc. Sometimes, there are even thoughts of suicide when the feeling of alientation from the youngster's own being and from the outer world becomes too great.

Mental changes take place too. The mental capacities increase noticeably and the child develops a facility for more abstract thinking so that he can come to terms with such concepts as liberty and justice. Memory improves and analytical and critical skills develop. This development commences as early as the tenth to the eleventh years of life (the biquintile of Saturn and the moon) but expands more fully at fourteen or fifteen.

With the onset of puberty, individual character traits and talents become more apparent and are revealed in the changed interests. Out of school a vital interest develops in all sorts of things in which one can give full rein to one's inclinations, and this can become a source of conflict between the personal interests and the heavier demands made by teachers at this stage of school life. One consequence may be laziness in class, not so much on account of the state of health, mental inability, home circumstances or the social environment, but more on account of resentment at having to spend time doing lessons when the mind is set on doing something else. This laziness, which is often encountered in the more intelligent teenagers is not equally distributed between boys and girls. Girls suffer from it less than boys do at this time of life, generally speaking. Anyway, when personal interests are cultivated, the ability to concentrate on school activities decreases.

The inclination to introversion and introspection given by the inconjunct aspects, is also seen in the attitude toward friendships displayed by the child during this period. Until about the twelfth year of life, being part of a group assumes considerable importance. The child plays with his friends because it is fun and not because he is particularly interested in the friends themselves. Friendship is still completely concerned with external things. This changes with the arrival of puberty. First of all, there is the withdrawn phase and the feeling of being friendless. Then the child looks not so much for lots of friends but for a 'special friend', the friend who will understand him and can share his secrets and experiences. This feature is very evident at that time in life when the moon and Saturn are within 'orbs' of their opposition aspects and it can last for several years.

This process of forming one's own identity, with all its crises and attendant lack of balance, is an indispensable part of the child's development towards adulthood. By analyzing the individual horoscope, we can further elucidate what the child is going through. Such an analysis will alert the parents and others in charge of the child to possible difficulties during the identity-forming process. Such difficulties have become known as an 'identity foreclosure' in the jargon employed by writers of current psychological literature, that is to say the attempt to fix oneself up with an identity before one is ready for it. Another popular term is 'negative identity', meaning the identification of oneself with any trend no matter what, simply to gain a feeling of identity. In the latter case, the youngster often feels that he has absolutely no identity, is of no importance, and yet does not care for the identity more or less imposed on him by his family and immediate circle. The negative identity consists for the child in identifying himself with the exact opposite of what is expected of him. If nothing else, it gives him a sense of being 'someone'. He prefers to be identified with delinquents and drop-outs rather than have no identity at all.

The other possibility of unbalanced adjustment to these

critical circumstances is the first-mentioned case, in which the child assumes an identity too early; a state of affairs regularly encountered in a pseudo-adult teenager. The process of experimenting with various rôles, with all its associated uncertainty, may be avoided if the teenager prematurely attaches himself to one or another set of standards and values. He often remains loyal to these standards without subjecting them to a critical analysis, in spite of further experience. A young person of this type often starts to plan his life at the age of sixteen or seventeen, usually under the influence of the aims and values of his parents or of his immediate circle of acquaintances. He seems to be free from the great uncertainties that go with forming an identity, and therefore looks to be more settled and well-balanced than his contemporaries. In reality, he has still failed to take an independent decision, and this failure is standing in the way of the formation of his own personality. The unfortunate individual enters a career that nine times out of ten proves unsuitable and is trapped in an early marriage before he has learnt to call his soul his own. The upshot is that the second crisis, at some time between the ages of twenty-eight and thirty, will bear on him all the harder. It is much more disturbing to him than it is to the person who has fought his battles when he was fifteen.

When Saturn and the moon once more form an inconjunct aspect with their radical positions, at the age of seventeen or thereabouts, there are further changes in the development of the character. The more internally directed crisis has an external aspect: the adolescent has an increasing urge to measure himself against anything in his life that has a fixed form. This has mainly to do with the expansion of his individual qualities; a process which began at the start of puberty and became noticeable around the age of fourteen when Uranus made its first sextile with its radical place. Some two years later, when the growing child is about seventeen years old, this planet forms a quintile with its own place. At this stage creative form-giving to the new characteristics and the new identity are central. At the same time, group interests re-appear. The period of introversion is left behind and the older teenager joins in with others sharing the same interests as himself. Political youth associations and societies with a certain world view become increasingly important to him. The adolescent is prepared to make a complete commitment to his ideals; he stands up for the dispossessed and for underprivileged social groups and becomes a member of bodies which preach reformation. Another mode of expression of this tendency, and one that is less welcome to society, is the decision to join a gang of juvenile criminals or vandals.

Sixteen also marks the end of compulsory education; a freedom for which society expects in return that the individual concerned will start to stand on his own two feet. This responsibility is not always immediately appreciated by the youngster.

The following sesquiquadrate of the moon and Saturn around eighteen or nineteen years of age brings the last spasm of this identity crisis. The adolescent enters the world with greater experience and knowledge and with an acquired or, at least, with an assumed identity. This is the time of life when many young people go into lodgings. It is generally assumed that they now know what they are doing. The adolescent finds a place in society, either by taking a job or by becoming a student. The fact that the aspect is a sesquiquadrate reveals that some tensions are involved, but proficiency is quickly gained in the new rôle, and so, the worst pressures on the inner side of life are fairly quickly relieved and life itself follows a more flexible course. From the nineteenth to the twentieth years Saturn and the moon make a trine to their own places. This is a relatively easy period when the individual has the feeling of being well in control of his own life.

The inclination to break away from old situations begins to assume a more concrete form at the age of twenty-one when Uranus makes a square with its radical position. A strong feeling of independence makes itself noticed. The individual wants as little interference as possible from others in his own affairs. Once again there is an interest in joining ideological groups. Non-personal values can play a part in the life of the individual for some considerable time and he entertains the wish to serve and help humanity in a disinterested manner. Meanwhile he proceeds with his studies or career and, gradually, the conflict between what he wants to do and what is expected by society comes into the open.

When Saturn and the moon again make a square with their positions in the natal horoscope, this tension between personal wishes and what is expected by those around can grow into a longing to abandon old patterns. This time the individual is much more conscious of his own wishes and has a vague feeling that there is much to life than what his immediate environment has to offer. It is at this age that many people have visions that they are going to die when they are about thirty years old. They have the unconscious knowledge that around the age of thirty we pass through a crisis when we have to decide whether to continue on the beaten track or to give our innermost needs their head. The changes undergone by the individual during this period may be viewed as a minor psychic death; it is a dying of old factors to make room for the successful development of the new.

Shortly after this period however, there follows a more easy-going time when both heavenly bodies make a quintile and then a sextile to their radical positions and, in this period of life from around twenty-three to twenty-five years of age, many people forget their first feelings of dissatisfaction with the existing situation. Productivity and creativity, both in the profession and in hobbies, can revive at this time with a consequent increase in self-reliance. Yet, this very peaceful period is only the calm before the storm.

The Return of the Moon and Saturn

The semi-square made by Saturn when the individual is about twenty-six, heralds the return of inner tensions and, in essence, forms the prelude to the first great crisis in life suffered by the individual. The crisis occurring at fourteen to fifteen years of age represented, in the development of the individual, the formation of the Ego and of a more conscious 'I' feeling. This fresh crisis, the first symptoms of which appear around the twenty-sixth year, signifies that the individual is faced with conscious choice based on his sense of uniqueness. It is a crisis involving the *Ego*.

At this time of life, the moon and Saturn begin to diverge from one another in their course round the horoscope. On average, we see that the secondary moon makes an aspect with its radical position sooner than Saturn makes the same aspect. The experience and content (the moon) comes first, and the pouring of the new contents into a fixed mould (Saturn) comes later. Nevertheless, the two heavenly bodies do not get completely out of step and the difference between them does not eventually amount to more than some six years during a life-span of eighty-four years or so. Because of the relatively slight discrepancy in their circuit times and because Saturn has a retrograde motion from time to time, allowance has to be made for the individual differences affecting this general rule. They may be safely ignored, however, in a survey such as this.

Real adulthood occurs between the ages of twenty-seven and thirty, when the moon and Saturn return to their birth positions in quick succession. The first cycle has been completed of these planets which symbolize the psychic factors enabling man to give shape to his earthly life. All possible aspects have now been made for the first time. To a large extent, the things mentioned so far have happened unconsciously, but all experiences and feelings are stored up in that layer of the human psyche termed the personal unconscoius. The usual lessons have been learned and a place has been won in the social system. In great measure, the rôle of the real parents in the life of the individual has been played out. The first trine now made by Uranus to its radical place is analogous to the psychological process of breaking loose (willy-nilly) from the parents and from the mode of life advocated by them. As was stressed earlier, the process of freeing oneself from the parental influence on one's inner life is an extremely important but usually a painful one. This painful aspect is not so much related to any squabbles, difficulties and misunderstandings between parents and child, but rather to the fact that the individual now feels that he is on his own and bears full responsibility for all his actions. His own identity is very much felt in these critical years; above all, that part of the personality which is not in harmony with the accepted norms and values, with accepted social behaviour or with the current living conditions becomes very evident. The impulse towards self-realization is innate in everybody and is in full flower at this time of life, but not everybody is equally well equipped to handle it, hence this is the period when there is a high incidence of unexpected events such as sudden changes of study or career, sudden marital difficulties and separations and, in short, a general tendency to make a break with whatever belongs to the past and to make a fresh start with what one wants to do as an individual. The person is no longer so prepared to do what is required of him. It is a time when many of us feel misunderstood, lost and hopeless. Some, in despair, contemplate suicide or even commit suicide when they are at their wits end.

At this point the individual faces a choice: whether to go on and live his life in his own way or to remain content to live by accepted standards and sacrifice for ever the chance of developing a unique part of his personality. This choice is not always made by the conscious mind. For some the step is taken completely consciously; others slip much less consciously into a new situation. In this connection, Carl Jung says that there also exists a state of consciousness in which the unconsciousness of a person preponderates as a consciousness in which awareness is the main feature. Moreover, he lays great stress on the decisive rôle played by the consciousness concerned, and on the associated possibility that this consciousness can provide an insight into the life situation. (This does not alter the fact that Jung attached as much importance to expressions of the unconscious in the shape of dreams, associations etc.)

These crisis years, when the individual is driven from within in an independent direction, can prove very trying to people who are set on clinging to what they have. Saturn can then represent a painful learning process and can bring with it an inescapable feeling of loneliness. On the other hand, the crisis can strip away unnecessary frills and those forms which are unsuited to the individual. This is helped by Uranus, which happens to be playing a leading rôle in the psyche at this time with its impulse towards freedom and the transcending of out-dated structures.

On the one hand, we see those who set themselves against everything new and strange and cling desperately to the past during this crisis. On the other hand, there are others who suddenly jettison the tried and trusted and are prepared to entertain only what is fresh and unfamiliar. We are quoting the two extremes, of course. The first is an example of the refusal to face the future and the second an example of deliberate alienation from the past. Both attitudes are unbalanced and are likely to be followed by an unconscious psychic reaction. They may both be characterized as a temporary relief by a narrowing of the consciousness, but the value of this crisis for the developing individual is that through the play of opposites or polarities, both in the inner man and in circumstances, a deeper insight will be gained and a wider frame of reference found. Gerhard Adler has this to say about what goes on under the surface in this whole development,

> It is only the person who fully accepts life with all its associated complications and conflicts, who grows into a living awareness that can give him fresh insights into his possibilities. Only through life-experience can the individual gain this awareness, and it is the tragedy of the whole situation that experience is possible only as he separates himself from his collective roots ... He who runs away from life, that is to say tries to avoid the development of his own personality, is disintegrated by life itself.

In previous chapters we have already seen how very much human beings are involved in urges and instinctive impulses present in the unconscious, which always cause some sort of trouble when they are excessively repressed and are thwarted rather than used in some form of development. When Gerhard Adler refers to the development of a man's own personality, he is talking about the same thing that Jung calls the 'individual process'. In its totality, this is really a spontaneous, natural and autonomous process within the psyche. It is present in us all, even though we are mostly unaware of it. To the extent that it is not restrained, limited or muffled by any disorder, it is, as a 'process of ripening or development', the psychic parallel of the growth and ageing of the body. This process of individuation usually takes place (when nature is allowed to have her way) in two stages, corresponding to the two halves of life. The first stage, which lasts until the forty-second year on average, is mainly concerned with adaptation to external circumstances and, in this, the first cycle of the moon and Saturn represents the learning phase. The second stage is concerned with the deepening of life and shedding the superficial.

With the arrival of the second cycle, the individual must learn to work in his own way with the material that has been acquired; he must extend his life further and must give himself further form in the social sphere etc. On the first return of the moon and Saturn to their own places in the horoscope, the time is ripe for the individual to pay heed to the innate impulse to self-realization; still however on the outer plane, on this first occasion of the return. In addition, the individual is faced with the problem of the unconscious, now that his parents as such have little further influence, of giving new forms to the father and mother archetypes present in the unconscious and of transcending them. The second cycle of the moon and Saturn is occupied with this process.

The Years Before the Change of Life

After the years in which the big crisis results in the adoption or otherwise of a new direction in life, there is a brief period of respite, that of the semi-sextile of the moon and Saturn with their radical positions. Shortly afterwards, at around the age of thirty-three, another semi-square is formed. The two psychic factors we are studying again undergo a strain within the psyche and this can imply various things.

From the time of the first return of the moon and Saturn, it becomes more difficult to say precisely what further tendencies lie concealed in the development of the individual, because the man himself decides if and how he will process his inner tensions and whether he will make a choice that is in harmony with his inner make-up. If, however, he makes a choice that is in conflict with his inner make-up, he will create a source of tensions which can later bring him nearer to his inner path in life. In the final analysis, it is out of differences that consciousness arises.

The process of individuation is admittedly an innate psychic posibility, but developing the personality is no bed of roses – it represents a curse as much as a blessing. It is a blessing because the person learns to live more harmoniously on the basis of his greater understanding, and a curse because this inner enrichment is hard-won. Jolande Jacobi writes in *The Psychology of C.G. Jung* 'The initial consequence is that the individual deliberately and inevitably breaks free from the situation of being nothing more than a face in the unthinking crowd. However, what is implied is not only isolation but also faith in his own way. He alone becomes a personality who, aware of his inner destination, sets out for it in a positive manner.' It is hardly surprising that the majority of people shrink from the tensions and the unavoidable difficulties associated with this process of gaining awareness, and therefore choose the line of least resistance and confine themselves to coping with their biological and material needs. Many are absorbed in looking for 'happiness' and it never occurs to them that happiness (defined as pleasurable sensations which are as continuous and as strong as possible) was not the end in view when man was created. The true purpose of life is a task that goes on until the end of life, namely a development of the whole personality which is as complete as possible. This produces something of imperishable and inestimable value: inner peace and, with it, the highest form of 'happiness'.

The moment when the moon and Saturn form their semi-square, means, for those who have paid due heed to their own inner promptings, a continuation of this process. This is often carried out in a somewhat militant manner, showing clearly how resolute the person is in becoming himself. It is the time when one discovers that there is no longer any turning back and that one must proceed along the chosen way. For those who are not too well settled, this semi-square aspect is a moment when they are no longer equal to the strain, especially when there is a new life-style and increased responsibility. There is a great danger that such people will relapse into the patterns with which they were familiar before the crisis at the age of twenty-seven to thirty. This reversion to the past means, all too often, that lives which were once so full of promise stagnate and show little further development. Many folk who, up to this point, seemed very progressive turn out to be conventional and even reactionary.

The years that follow now present a picture of considerable inner repose and creativity. Many people at this time are fully occupied with their career, their family and raising their children; in short, with the needs of the moment. Carl Jung calls this an essential phase in human development. First of all we have to know how to perform adequately in the external world, in our job for example; the deepening of the inner life comes later in the second half of life. This comparatively easy period falls in the time when Saturn and the moon make a sextile and then a quintile to their radical positions. The age at which this happens is from about thirty-four to thirty-six years old. Now is the time to develop further and to become accustomed to the way of life that has just been entered. Even those who have reverted to their old ways also experience this calm and creativity, but there are things lying dormant that can create a serious crisis when they reach the age of forty-five or thereabouts – the change of life.

At the age of thirty-six to thirty-seven there is another period of tension when Saturn and the moon reach a position which is in square aspect to their own places in the natal horoscope. This is the time when the difficulties and faults which have been inherent in the way of life so far adopted make themselves felt, and the barriers which have been erected over past years have to be surmounted. It is also the time when those problems which (whether consciously or not) have been ignored, cry out for some solution. The root of the trouble may lie as much in the home as in work. Difficulties may crop up in the family because the children see too little of their father because he is under a constant pressure of work; hanging on to the job that has been won can bring many headaches. The square aspect indicates that an attempt must be made to get right down to the psychic sources of tensions and whatever has so far been overlooked; then there will be some hope of doing better in future. Anything without good use in the environment and everything effete in the psyche will need to be swept aside. Some people may have a nervous breakdown at this particular age. For many others, however, it is the time of life when they can expand their range of activities.

At about thirty-five years of age and after, the factors represented by the planet Uranus gain greater prominence. The need is felt for further change, for breaking with the old in order to savour the new and also for emphasizing one's own individuality. The aspect made by Uranus with its natal position around the thirty-fifth year of age is the inconjunct or quincunx aspect, on the way to the opposition aspect at approximately forty-two. This is how Carl Jung describes the process preceding a new crisis in life, that is, the change of life:

In the lifespan between thirty-five and forty, we observe preparations for a significant change in human psyche. At first this change takes place in an unconscious and scarcely perceptible manner. Even indirect symptoms of the change are barely present. It gradually wells up from the human unconscious. Often there is a gradual alteration in the character on the person, in other cases certain traits can be displayed which were missing in childhood.

During the period between the first return of the moon and Saturn to their places at birth and the years occupied by the change of life in the middle of life, the individual becomes more successful at forming opinions and, consequently, at gaining a more influential position in society. It begins to look as if the individual has 'got the hang of things' at last, is steering the right course through life and has the right ideals and principles. The danger introduced by these personal convictions and ideas is that the one who holds them will, more often than not, regard them as being of general application, and so not only can a certain rigidity of attitude creep in with regard to himself and others but also there is a tendency to regard these ideas as unassailable in this still changing world. A further consequence is that he is not inclined to let go of these values of his when his psyche changes and, in the relatively placid period between the ages of thirty-eight and forty, it is possible that his values, his moral attitude and other opinions will crystallize to such an extent that they will stand in the way of further individual development. It is unfortunately quite probable that the person concerned will become set in an almost inflexible pattern of thought and behaviour.

The moon and Saturn form trines to their natal positions in this period. After all the tensions of the square aspect, the individual feels much better and many people at this time of life still consider that life has much to offer. A few merely sense the currents in the unconscious part of their psyches, which can emerge in their dreams and share in the preparation for a difficult though very creative and formative period for the personality. Once again the individual is confronted with the choice of either coming to terms with his inner development or falling back on the values that held good for his more youthful days.

The Change of Life

Although the symptoms of the menopause in the woman appear on average only between the ages of forty-seven and forty-eight, the first signs of crisis present themselves in the psyche much sooner than this, at the age of about forty-two. These mental symptoms are by no means restricted to the female sex. On the contrary, men as well as women undergo similar psychic changes between their fortieth and forty-seventh years and for both sexes this period well deserves the name 'change of life'. In what follows, we shall mainly be talking about the psychic changes associated with this time of life rather than about the physiological details of the menopause.

Not everybody consciously experiences great psychic changes at the change of life. Roughly speaking, we can distinguish two groups (although, of course, there are intermediate sub-groups). Those in group one gradually adapt to another outlook on life and are scarcely aware of the inner changes and merely experience this period as a difficult one. Things are not as easy as usual but they do not enquire into the reason. Those in group two are more alive to what is happening to them and suffer from it much more, generally speaking. They are, however, in a position to learn a great deal, especially in regard to their inner drives and wishes, and thus can arrive at a more aware and harmonious outlook (one of the aims of the individuation process that is inherent in life).

It is hard to say how someone will react to the inner changes. A lot depends on the conscious attitude and on the way in which previous experiences have been assimilated or otherwise; even, indeed, on whether or not there has been an ability or willingness to assimilate them. The less prepared a person is for this change, the more he will be affected by it, provided of course that it does in fact occur and that the individual does not stay stranded in an infantile or adolescent state and end up with a smouldering, chronic neurosis.

At the end of its third decade and the commencement of its fourth, life usually runs along fixed lines in every respect. The family is growing up, the social position is pretty sound, the individual is established in his job or profession and he has a place in the world. In short, the phase of giving external form to life nears completion. It is at this time of life that people ask themselves why on earth they have been doing what they have been doing and what further purpose their lives will serve and so on.

By degrees, the feeling is gained that there must be more to life than simply satisfying basic needs. The sesquiquadrates of the moon and Saturn to their radical positions are indicative of this duality, which is further deepened at the age of about forty-one, when a biquintile and an inconjunct aspect follow one another in quick succession. With the growth of inner uncertainty comes the realization that so little has been experienced in life and so much has been missed.

There is also a noticeable reduction in the sexual urge around the forty-second year of life, a phenomenon that is closely linked with the biological and psychological development of the human being. The feelings of devaluation and anxiety which the reduction in potency or desire can arouse are often the source of all sorts of over-compensations at this time of life. There are spasmodic attempts to prove that one still belongs to the younger generation, that one is still a force to be reckoned with, that one is still the epitome of strength, beauty, youth etc. Not for nothing is this period called the 'second youth'. Those who up to this time have striven to take their cue from the standards set by society, have a fresh opportunity to be more themselves and to follow their own bent more: Uranus is in opposition to itself.

Owing both to the feelings of uncertainty – with all the resulting over-compensation – and to the inclination to pay heed to that inner voice that speaks of continued development, a person can abandon his course for quite a while and drift rudderless in an ocean of vague feelings and anxieties. The increasingly pressing questions concerning the meaning of his life and the purpose of his own activities makes a considerable contribution to this state of affairs. The usual consequences are psychic and psychosomatic disturbances, diseases of all kinds, divorce, change of occupation, changing house, financial losses etc. These are only a few of the many happenings which occur more or less suddenly at this time of life. If little difficulty has been experienced in the crisis at puberty and later in the crisis around the first return of the moon and Saturn, there is a good chance that at the age of forty-two or so the individual will be thrown completely off balance. That is to say, when the Ego is too little developed, he will have the feeling that his activities are subject to arbitrary and uncontrollable impulses, in spite of the fact that he is well aware of the whole situation. If, on the contrary, the Ego is very firmly anchored in the psyche, the person concerned finds in this period that all the repressed factors of the personal unconscious combine to form a single and significant counterpart to the unbalanced conscious psyche. This can result in psychic disturbances which are in many cases quite serious. It is at this time of life that one pays the price for choosing a negative identity or for choosing an identity too early on in adolescence.

The symptoms of the crisis can show themselves for years and may even get worse around the age of forty-four. This is the time when the moon and Saturn make an opposition to their own radical positions. The form-giving capacity in man, already under attack from the destructive tendencies of Uranus in opposition to itself, comes under heavy pressure in these years. The father and mother archetypes start to play a new rôle internally. Ideally, they should no longer be attached to the real parents at this time of life; in many instances, however, this is not so. Carl Jung found time and time again that people tend to identify themselves with their youth for longer when their real parents are still living than when they are dead. It is when the parents are still alive that the above-mentioned symptoms of crisis are more than likely to occur even later in life so that the deferred psychic process can take place. 'I have mainly observed this in cases where the father survived for a long time. The father's death then has the effect of a hurried, almost catastrophic transition to maturity,' says Jung.

The father and mother archetypes, which contain in essence the duality of life in one's own psyche, have called for gradual transformation in the preceding years. Nevertheless, this transformation can take place only when one knows how to find a balanced aim in the second half of life – a problem which seems to epitomize the crisis. The psychic changes which have been going on inwardly now break through into consciousness, with associated nervous disorders, destructive inclinations, reduction in activities and the feeling that everything is 'all for nothing'. Depressions, increased instability, anxieties and (in the man) problems over potency are, as typical symptoms, all made worse when one is not prepared to face the fact that one's youthful ideals no longer fit in with the conditions of life. When one enters life's second half the problems to be faced are different from the problems of the first. In the second half of life new inner conditions are encountered. The concept 'change of life' means 'change' in the most literal sense. It is the conversion of an outgoing attitude to a more inward-looking one. The first and second parts of life complement each other. The individual development in the first half of life is absolutely necessary to bring about a fair degree of balance in the second half of life. Schopenhauer once compared the difference between the two halves of life to the appearance of a piece of embroidered cloth. In the first half we have the pretty, coloured front side and in the second half of life we have the reverse side – less colourful but often more instructive, because the interrelationship of the threads is then apparent.

Carl Jung's example is the daily course of the sun; an example given by him after he has first demonstrated that the basis and cause of all the problems in this transitional period are to be found in a deep-rooted, particular change within the psyche. In the early morning the sun rises up out of the ocean of night (our unconscious) and surveys the brightening world that lies before him. He slowly climbs an increasing expanse of earth with his beams (we become increasingly aware of ourselves and of the world). We may imagine that, if the sun were a person, he would have a growing sense of his own importance during his morning ascent and would regard his highpoint at noon as the main aim. But, immediately on culmination, his path begins to descend and, just as the rising of the sun forms a contrast to his setting, so the values and ideals in the period following the high point in human life are the opposite of those which were prized in youth. This reversal in the psyche goes hand in hand with physical alterations. But, all too often, neurotic disturbances occur in adults after these transitional years because they persist in cherishing youthful ideals at a time of life when these are no longer appropriate. In Western society, it is almost quite commonplace for the older generation to compete with the younger in certain fields of activity and, as Jung says, '... the

mother seems anxious to be taken for her daughter's younger
sister ...'.

The source of all the difficulties encountered in these years
is the drastic nature of this about-face, although some will feel
the change more acutely than others. Here too, it must be
pointed out that the horoscope should be progressed as a
whole, because it is only the individual progressions that can
provide information concerning the course of the crisis. Yet,
even without benefit of progressions, it can be stated that the
period around forty-four years of age is a decisive one for the
setting of future objectives and, in spite of difficulties, can in
all cases be a period of self-realization in which tensions will
be greatly reduced after the age of forty-six or forty-seven.
After the inconjunct aspects have become exact at
approximately this time, the individual goes on once more to
experience the effects of the biquintiles and trines of the moon
and Saturn to their radical places, interrupted briefly by the
influence of a sesquiquadrate. At the age of forty-seven or
thereabouts, transiting Jupiter has completed its fourth
circuit, and so a new social period with new demands
coincides with the sesquiquadrate just mentioned. This
coincidence can signify tensions during the female
menopause, but perhaps it is better to see it as the rounding
off externally of the psychic transition process than to see it as
an independent phenomenon. Much of what the individual
goes on to experience in life depends on the way in which this
transition has been assimilated and accepted; a transition
termed by Charlotte Bühler, a 'change in dominance' – a
switch to a fresh rule of life.

Growth towards the Second Return of the Moon and
Saturn

As the moon and Saturn advance towards their trines with
their radical places, a period is entered in which the inner
growth accomplished in the past year is stablized and often
seems to lead the individual to come to terms with life. He
feels an inner strength and is able to get a better response from
those around him; always assuming, of course, that he has
been able and willing to assimilate what has gone before and
has not been trapped at an earlier stage. The inconjunct
aspect of the planet Uranus to its own radical position can

indicate one of two things in this connection. For the person who has come to a halt somewhere in his development, a fresh feeling of tension regarding his own personality will give a sense of dissatisfaction, a sense of emptiness and of being unfulfilled. There is an inkling that something remains to be done or should be done which it may no longer be possible to do. The inner urge towards self-realization can confront such a person in all sorts of ways with his own misunderstood stage of growth.

The successive trines made by the moon and Saturn may bring some solace but also the danger that the individual will rest content with an obsolete attitude to life. The second possibility inherent in this Uranus aspect is that of creative frustration. Here the individual makes headway along his chosen path and braves any resistance which may present itself. In this instance, the trines of the moon and Saturn to their own radical positions mirror the inner sense of repose and provide a firm basis for further development. Many people in this age-group have the renewed impulse to get out and about, not so much with the idea of letting things slide, but for the sake of conversation, an exchange of opinions and the opportunity to propagate their own ideas.

At the age of about forty-nine, Pluto makes a quintile with its radical position, and this can indicate various things, which largely depend for their expression on the person's stage of growth. As the aspect of ability, the quintile means that, in this period, the disposition can be over-emphasized. Pluto always stands for the struggle for power, among other things; it represents the will. Inner transformations can take place in a subtle way and the individual becomes more open to 'other realities' whether he is aware of it or not. This is connected with the fact that, at this stage, he approaches the second return of the moon and Saturn to their radical positions, and finds himself increasingly confronted with the end of life. Topics such as death and the hereafter become more important. The Pluto aspect can do as much to help one solve this problem as it can do to aggravate it. In the first case, we see that a more receptive attitude to other realities can support the individual and reconcile him to his inevitable demise so indissolubly bound up with birth and life. In the other case, inner fear and uncertainty can make him clutch at some religious or pseudo-religious creed, which he proceeds to defend fanatically. Often, the greater the fear and uncertainty, the greater the fanaticism. We are not trying to imply that everyone in this period who has a view of life based on religious convictions is seized with an inner fear. On the contrary. It quite frequently happens that it is mainly those who feel an emptiness in their souls and who feel there must be more to life but have failed to find it, who go in search of some marvel or other. As soon as they think they have discovered it they are inclined to treat it as the one and only truth which it is their duty to both embrace and promote. People in such a frame of mind often become the chela of some guru, the disciples of some 'prophet' or of anyone who preaches something 'new' with intense conviction, even if it is a rehash of an old faith. Whatever form it takes, the fanaticism is often striking at this time of life.

The person who has managed to keep pace internally with the events of life and has, in fact, gone his own way at the age of thirty, may very well find that, by the time he is fifty, others are taking him as a sort of example because they themselves have paid no attention to the inner urge to self-realization.

This whole process takes place when the moon and Saturn move on to the following square aspect. The tensions entailed mean for the creative man that he must do more work on his own individuality. For those, however, who have fallen behind in the routine affairs of daily life, the square often signifies putting on a mask or erecting a façade, although doing so affords no protection against the growing despondency within. The prospect now facing the more senior citizen is the end of his working life and the status of a pensioner. After he has been pensioned off, a gaping void opens up before him unless he has learnt to be himself and to fill his life with other interests besides those of bread-winning or winning prestige. As a prelude to the coming years, the individual will learn with ever increasing clarity that – notwithstanding the lesson of the first twenty-eight years that led to the development of a genuine individuality – there is more to life than the possession of one's own individuality. With this realization, he reaches the phase which rounds off the external side of the individuation process, a process that will still occupy a considerable time.

The square aspect is formed between the fiftieth and fifty-third years, a time during which Uranus moves from the biquintile aspect to the sesquiquadrate: old ideas must give way to new insights and experiences. The square tests the validity of one's opinions for this period in life and, at the same time, any tensions which arise draw attention to facets of the character which have so far been given little or no chance to express themselves. We refer here not merely to factors which have been repressed but to genuine abilities and talents.

Assimilation of the factors which come to light during the formation of the square, takes place in the following period when the moon and Saturn first make sextiles. Internalization is a key word for the whole period after the square. Often there are no longer any great external changes in the person's circumstances. Internally, however, life can be subject to considerable changes and refinements. For those who are strongly attached to ideals and opinions which are no longer appropriate to this time of life, and for those whose self-image has fossilized, so to speak, at an earlier stage of development, this period is a very trying one. Even during the sextile aspect, the feeling of unrest caused by unconscious reactions to the rigid conscious attitude remains.

The human psyche always strives for balance and, if its equilibrium is disturbed, there is a onesided emphasis on one aspect (in this case on the conscious attitude) which means that the individual concerned is no longer completely at rest even in those periods which are running relatively smoothly. It is these people in particular who can fall prey to factors in their own unconscious at the moment when the moon and Saturn return again to their radical positions, so completing their second cycle: the critical years.

The Second Return and Old Age: a Period of Importance in Life

In the period from fifty-five to sixty years of age, a number of significant astrological tendencies follow one another in a relatively short time. The return of the moon to its radical place is followed by the first trine of Neptune to its own radical position; then, at about the age of fifty-six, Uranus makes a second trine with itself. Finally, Saturn and Jupiter each make a conjunction with their radical places at some time near fifty-nine years of age. The symptoms of crisis associated with this concourse of aspects make their appearance when Saturn forms a semi-square with its radical place; which happens around about the time when the moon makes a conjunction. (It will no doubt be remembered that, later in life, the aspects of these two heavenly bodies begin to get out of synchronization).

At this stage, ageing can be sensed as a threat. The physical signs that point to approaching old age are unmistakable and every effort to keep up with the younger generation will be recognized in advance as a waste of time. Feelings of uncertainty over the question, 'what next?' will all too often induce the individual to hark back to ideas and values he ought to have outgrown. Here too, just as at the change of life, feelings of uncertainty and anxiety can arise over the sense that what has been attained is not all that it should have been. The result is a spirit of dissatisfaction. There is the feeling that life should have been different or more fulfilling. Solid achievements are often brushed aside as unimportant and of little value. Just as in the change of life, sudden separations seem to occur at this point and more people put an abrupt end to all sorts of current situations. Sometimes the person falls sick as a negative reaction to a situation which is too burdensome. This is a time of life when many a false step is made and one wants to make a fresh start and a clean break with what has gone before. One is beset with fears concerning old age too.

The period now commencing is essentially that time in which the internalized attitude to life and its shaping become important. The change to internalization took place as far back as the change of life, under a certain degree of compulsion. The phase begins in which one gradually attaches less value to external phenomena and pays more attention to inner processes. The crisis at the second return of the moon and Saturn is based on the realization that even the fact that one is an individual, more or less different from all other human beings, is not the be-all and the end-all. In the process of becoming his mature self as a unique being, an individual becomes more and more alienated from the natural processes within himself and from his instinctive drives. At this time of life he enters a situation in which he feels both his instinctive drives (which were still relatively important in the first cycle) and his conscious individuality which he learnt to develop in the course of the second cycle. These two psychic factors are contrary to one another and there is a great danger that one will be torn between conflicting interests and feelings which, at first sight, seem irreconcilable. It is the first trine made by Neptune to its own place that affords a clue as to what will follow. This aspect symbolizes a psychic factor that will accompany human growth from that moment onward. The collective psyche assumes greater importance and, in this crisis, the person can come to the realization there are higher values than those of the Ego and things of greater importance than the creative self-expression characteristic of the second cycle of the moon and Saturn. Spiritual values, whether or not linked with Christian teaching, can now fully enter experience. Only now is that phase reached in which the promise held out by Neptune in the natal horoscope can be redeemed and made good. The personally and socially aware attitude to life can overflow into a humanitarian interest in world events without a strong sense of involvement in them. This development of a clearly recognizable character with a much more impersonal, universal set of values and tolerant attitude in which the individual attaches a more relative worth to himself, begins in the phase of the second return of the moon and Saturn.

It is certainly not everyone, however, who goes on to this universal and inclusive side of the psychic factor symbolized by Neptune. Many, as already mentioned, fall into an attitude in which a selection of sentimental youthful memories are recalled to help them relive past glories and vague ideals are cherished and extolled. There may even be a relapse into second childhood. How the things mentioned develop depends on what has been learnt and assimilated in the preceding years of life.

Many of us do not live long enough to see the end of the third cycle of the moon and Saturn. In this cycle, also, there are critical and quiet periods, although these do not upset the even tenor of existence so much as they did in the previous cycles. When the Ego knows how to keep up with the inner psychic progress, it will not be so vulnerable because it has learned to see itself in a relative light. It is now extremely important to bring the conscious part of the psyche into balance with the unconscious part so as to stabilize the whole personality. 'This seems to be a preparation for death in the deepest sense of the word. For death is no less important than birth and is just as inseparable a part of life. If we would only understand her aright, nature herself takes us in her sheltering arms. The older we grow the less the outer world has to say to us and the more it loses colour, sound and delight and the more insistently we are summoned and occupied by the inner world. In ageing, man steadily approaches the point where he flows back into the collective psyche from whence he emerged with so much difficulty as a child. And so the cycle of human life terminates meaningfully and harmoniously and the beginning and ending coincide. This has been symbolized from time immemorial by Ouroboros, the serpent with its tail in its mouth. If this task is brought to a successful conclusion, death must lose its terror and be accepted as a meaningful part of life. Allowance, however, must be made for the fact that even the fulfilment of the task confronting man in the first half of life seems, in itself, to be beyond the capacity of many, as can be gathered from the infantile adults we see around us everywhere; it is little to be wondered at, then, how few manage to round off their lives with full self-realization.' These words of Jolande Jacobi provide a brief summary of what is entailed in the final cycle of the moon and Saturn, which commences in the problem years between fifty-five and sixty and carries within it the possibility of eventual self-fulfilment by the individual.

Final Considerations

What has gone before may seem to suggest that the cycles of the moon and Saturn always carry the same message: grow further, release your hold on old and effete values and be receptive to the new but, above all, recognize the eternal law that *everything* in life changes. This appears to be a contradictory state of affairs as far as Saturn is concerned, since Saturn has always been the planet of stability and fixity. Looking at this fixity a little closer, we find that usually people try to preserve forms as they are out of fearfulness – another Saturn characteristic. When we master our fear of losing the old, we are in a position to take full advantage of the other side of Saturn, that is to say to profit by its ability to penetrate to the heart of any matter; in this case to our own essential nature, so that we are in a position to see ourselves more clearly. The Ego then becomes better defined. Saturn is the touchstone of the durable, and its cycles round the horoscope have the effect of unmasking and removing all that is not useful, not valuable and not permanent.

There is no need to be afraid of the cycles of the moon and Saturn (even though the emphasis has been laid on the crises in life, because these serve to highlight the course of life rather usefully). To the extent that this fear springs from incomprehension of the significance of these cycles, it is completely unfounded. Our growth is gradual. However, where our anxiety is created by a conscious resistance to growth, it is not the cycles as such that make us nervous but the special placement of 'fear-making' Saturn in the horoscope. It is fear that can numb us, and rob us of all initiative; yet Saturn also provides the impetus to go further. And so, we may petrify and shrivel in a caricature of our own past, but we can break the deadlock by a positive act of will and attain a new freedom. Too often, however, we are rigid and inert, too stick-in-the-mud and timorous. By clinging to what we dread losing we are unable to fully profit by our own inner response to Saturn's influence. As Liz Greene says: 'Saturn is the process of learning through pain, but it turns the frog into a prince.' Our father and mother images, Saturn and the moon, constantly encounter us on our path through life from various directions. The crises to which they are related are closely linked with the degree to which we can free ourselves of any complexes. This may be seen in the preceding sketch of the development of human life. The whole of life is a process of gaining in awareness and increasing in knowledge. Man, therefore, becomes really aware of things only with the lapse of time. Time is required for us to experience the difference between what was and what is. In a number of respects, experiences seem to come in greater and lesser cycles. Recognition of these cycles gives more understanding, in many cases, of the natural development of life. Deeper insight into life and its cycles reduces anxiety and, when this is reduced, more attention can be paid to coming to terms with inner events. By this process it is possible to recover from an overdose of fatalism. Insight into the whole life process makes it easier to discover the uniqueness of one's own being. Eventually, each measure of release from fatalism and fear means that the personality can become more balanced. In essence this is more or less the same as a balanced transcendence of the innate father and mother images. At this point we have come full circle to our starting point at the beginning of the chapter.

All life is a development from out of the collective unconscious and, having given shape to consciousness, it returns to what is now a conscious experience of the collective psychic factors. The child knows nothing as yet of life and its possibilities and has even less idea of the rôle played in its life by its parents, a rôle which it lets them play, so to speak, by projecting on them the inborn father and mother archetypes. Its further development during the cycles of the moon and Saturn eventually alters its attitude towards its real parents. This is a reflection of inner changes in form undergone by the unconscious factors involved. Separation from the parents or the death of the parents bring with them further possibilities for development of these primitive images which, having 'incarnated' in the parents, go on to assume more abstract forms. It is never possible to break free from these images; they belong to the innate equipment of the human race. The point of interest lies in just how an individual will give form to these archetypes which, as complementary to one another, have the potential to make his life creative.

In old age, the sharp polarization produced between the father and mother archetypes becomes somewhat blunted, even without benefit of a lifetime's experience. It is the Ego's polarization of personal factors and of the form it bestows on those factors, which creates the difference that maintains the current of psychic energy; just as a difference in level causes water to run downstream. This flow of energy is the motor and propulsive force behind the life and experience of man. Nevertheless, as man grows older, the Ego, relinquishing its claim to be the centre of the psyche, accepts a more legitimate and fitting function. The individual draws more upon the source of the collective psyche and, as all this occurs, the polarization, gradually weakens, and the stream of psychic energy often loses speed and force. Joy and sorrow do not rise to their former heights of feeling and, relatively speaking, the emotional life has a more even tenor. Thus, the 'way back' can be covered in full awareness. Mindful of the profound words of the Tao Teh King:

Tao brings forth one,
One brings forth two,
Two brings forth three,
Three brings forth the ten thousand things,
The ten thousand things bring forth the dark element without and the light element within.

We can postulate that, during his life, man first passes through a phase of external phenomena – the ten thousand things. It is in these phenomena that the duality of life is contained. We can experience a thing only when we have something with which to compare it. Light and dark, male and female, Father and Mother, everything is knowable only through its counterpart which completes it. The ten thousand things carry within them this difference between the dark principle and the light principle.

The forms in which the moon and Saturn express themselves in their cycles can enable us to experience this duality. The ten thousand things are experienced as such only through the psychic energy flow, named by the Tao Teh King 'three'. It is not possible for psychic energy to flow except when there is difference between two factors: 'Two brings forth three'. The difference between positive and negative, male and female etc. and the difference between moon and Saturn in their cyclic relationship, give the psychic energy the opportunity to maintain its flow and so to create a balance between the two factors – which, in my opinion, are the original primitive factors in man, lying at the very basis of his inner being. Then, as we work our way back, we can convert the 'One brings forth two' (out of the restored balance between the two contrasting entities – between the father and mother archetypes) to the very core of the matter: One. To us this means the Self, the life force, the divine spark or whatever else we wish to call that which harmoniously unites male and female, conscious and unconscious. Looked at from this point of view, death is the step taken by 'One' back to TAO.

Bibliography

Adler, Gerhard: *Studies in Analytical Psychology* (Hodder & Stoughton, London, 1969)

Greene, Liz: *Relating: An Astrological Guide to Living with Others on a Small Planet,* (Coventure Books, Denham, 1978)

Hone, Margaret E.: *The Modern Textbook of Astrology* (Fowler, Romford, 1961)

Jacobi, Jolande: *The Psychology of C.G. Jung* (Hodder & Stoughton, London, 1973)

Jung, Carl G.: *Analytical Psychology*, Collected Works, Vol. 7 (Routledge & Kegan Paul, London, 1966)

—— *The Archetypes and the Collective Unconscious*, Collected Works, Vol. 9 (Routledge & Kegan Paul, London, 1971)

—— *Civilization in Transition*, Collected Works, Vol. 10 (Routledge & Kegan Paul, London, 1964)

—— *Memories, Dreams and Reflections* (Fontana, London, 1964)

—— *Modern Man in Search of a Soul* (Routledge & Kegan Paul, London, 1933)

—— *Mysterium Coniunctionis*, Collected Works, Vol. 14 (Routledge & Kegan Paul, London, 1963)

—— *Psychology and Alchemy*, Collected Works, Vol. 12 (Routledge & Kegan Paul, London, 1968)

—— *Psychological Types*, Collected Works, Vol. 6 (Routledge & Kegan Paul, London, 1971)

—— *The Spirit in Art and Literature*, Collected Works, Vol. 15 (Routledge & Kegan Paul, London, 1966)

—— *The Structure and Dynamics of the Psyche*, Collected Works, Vol. 8 (Routledge & Kegan Paul, London, 1960)

—— *Symbols of Transformation*, Collected Works, Vol. 5 (Routledge & Kegan Paul, London, 1967)

—— *Synchronicity: An Acausal Connecting Principle* (Routledge & Kegan Paul, London, 1955)

Mayo, Jeff: *The Planets and Human Behaviour* (Fowler, Romford, 1972)

Neumann, Erich: *The Great Mother* (Routledge & Kegan Paul, London, 1963)

—— *The Origins and History of Consciousness* (Routledge & Kegan Paul, London, 1954)

Singer, June K.: *Boundaries of the Soul: The Practice of Jung's Psychology* (London, 1973)

Wilhelm, Richard: *The Secret of the Golden Flower* (Routledge & Kegan Paul, London, 1962)